M&A Basics

For People in a (BIG) Hurry!

Master the Latest Methods for Getting Top Dollar for Your Business

John D. Wagner

1StWest M&A Press
Colorado

CONTENTS

Wagner, John, D.

M&A Basics for People in a (Big) Hurry:
Master the Latest Methods for Getting Top Dollar for
Your Business

ISBN: 978-0-578-95287-1

Many of these chapters first appeared in slightly different forms in *LBM Journal, SBC Magazine,* and *Industrial Distribution* magazine.

First Edition

Printed in the USA

02, 03, 04, 05, 06, 07, 08, 09

For Ted Rieple

Second Shortest Preface Ever

This is the *second* shortest preface ever written. How do I know it's the second shortest preface ever written? Because I wrote the *first* shortest preface as an introduction to my previous book, *M&A Basics for People in a Hurry.*

Since I wrote that book – which I published in two editions – M&A has gotten hotter, richer and, well, BIG. Deals have gotten bigger, there's tons of liquidity (cash) sloshing around in the investment market, and there are more deals on the market, especially now that Baby Boomer business owners are reaching that age where they want to cash out. Our firm has never been busier, and that's saying something, given that our principals have closed more than $1 billion in deal values to date.

So, I've written a BIGGER book to bring you even more best-practices, tricks, and techniques for getting the highest values in the sale of your businesses. And (I couldn't help myself) I have taken time to tell a few "war stories" of how deals got done, crazy offers that were floated to buyers, and some of the exceptional characters I've met along the way. This book, *M&A Basics for People in a (BIG) Hurry,* expands on my previous writing, and the contents continues to be informed by lessons learned "on the street" from deals and engagements that our firm has completed.

One thing that *hasn't* gotten bigger is the time you have on your schedule. So, I've kept most chapters to under 800 words. Most of us read at 200 words a minute. So, except for the longer first chapter, these chapters can each be read in just five or so minutes.

Finally, this book is available for free to our clients; inquire at our firm's website: 1stWestMA.com or contact me directly.

There. Second shortest preface ever written. A promise kept.

"Success usually comes to those who are too busy to be looking for it." — Henry David Thoreau

Chapter 1

Considering Selling Your Business?

Here's How to Prepare

Most business owners who inquire about selling their business ask the same two opening questions.

1. "What metrics are used to determine the value of my business when a buyer is looking to purchase?"

2. "What are the top three or four steps I can take to maximize that value?"

All buyers value the same basic performance metrics of a company. These metrics are easy to identify, and once a business owner determines it's time to prepare for a sale, it is a relatively straightforward task to optimize the sale value of the company by focusing on these well-known metrics. That said, these metrics measure aspects of a business that cannot be changed overnight, and if you are selling your business, and these parts of your business need a tune-up, you should have a lead time of around six months to one year to get your house in order. Let's take a closer look.

Where to Focus?

During your preparation-for-sale period, focus on improving the productivity and performance of your business, both top line (gross revenues) and bottom line (net profit).

Potential buyers will scrutinize your financial statements for the last *three years* and look for continuous financial performance. Keep in mind that potential buyers are looking for continuous financial performance and will want to examine those three years of records. You will achieve the highest valuation when you show an improvement year-over-year. A business that books $15 million in business for each of the last three years with good net margins may be very attractive to you, the owner of that business, but the value of that company will be heightened if a buyer sees consistent, predictable year-over-year *growth* in addition to solid financial performance, typically measured by *percent EBITDA* (explained later).

The longer the track record of growth, the more you, the seller, could reasonably argue that a consistent growth trend could be expected to continue in future years. But more importantly, the value of the business could reflect this future growth *now* by achieving a premium valuation that prices in that growth.

It should come as no surprise that the old basics still matter. Buyers are looking for things:

1. A solid balance sheet with excellent A/R (showing little or no account dating and low delinquencies).

2. Good cash flow.

3. Control over operating expenses (OPEX), and good performance in terms of OPEX as a percent of sales.

4. Quality sustainable earnings, and a strong EBITDA margin compared to other companies in your sector.

These are among the primary drivers in the valuation process. It is these metrics that should be your top priorities during the preparation period.

"Well-Presented...Half Sold"

In addition to getting the financial aspects of the business in order, it is also essential that your financial performance be well-documented. Well-presented financial statements that use standardized GAAP methods of accounting will go a long way to giving your buyer confidence that you are running a high-performance company. Just having your financials in order can actually heighten values almost as much as solid earnings because the buyer will think: "Heck, if they've got their financials in such good shape, I'll bet the rest of the business is equally well cared for."

Furthermore, as you prepare for sale, an internal SWOT analysis (*Strengths, Weakness, Opportunities & Threats*) can be a useful tool in determining what aspects of the business need improvement. In fact, a potential buyer of your business will more than likely perform their own SWOT analysis, so you can only imagine how impressive it will be if you get ahead of the curve and perform your own SWOT analysis to show that you are working to improve the business, even as you prepare to sell it.

Within the SWOT analysis, S (Strengths) and W (Weaknesses) refer to internal factors in your company that you can control. O (Opportunities) and T (Threats) are typically outside the control of your business but directly impact your business.

Timing

Timing the sale of your business is based on many factors, but two are critical. You want to sell your business when it is doing well *and* the industry sector is healthy. Just as an unprofitable business has little value in a good economy, a company with historically strong earnings will not achieve its highest value if it is sold when the economy is on the decline or in the tank. If you work in a cyclical industry (and most of us do) and times are good now, you have to ask yourself: Am I prepared to wait out the next downturn, which could easily be a four-to-six-year cycle? Or should I sell now, knowing that the sale process will take around six months to a year to complete?

A solid economic environment that is at its peak, or even near its peak — on its way *up*, not on the way down! — is an ideal time to engage a mergers and acquisitions advisory team to help prepare your business and put it on the market to see what valuations you could achieve.

There are external factors, such as the overall economy, global events, and industry business cycles, which are not in your control, and it's probably a mark of prudence (and not stupidity) to take your exit in a safe business environment, even if you potentially leave a "little bit of money on the table."

For example: If your business is worth between 5x and 7x multiple of EBITDA today—that's a typical multiple range for many business sectors for an all-cash deal and valuations can go much higher with multi-year earnouts—that multiple can *easily* drop in a down cycle, where you would see a 5x multiple of EBITDA or lower. You would need to increase your EBITDA by 40% just to get back to a dollar valuation equal to the 7x multiple of EBITDA in an up-market cycle. Selling today at a 7x, even when you suspect you could achieve a higher value, would likely be a great move in retrospect if the economy were to constrict.

Valuations

Is your business special? Sure it is! Just like a homeowner who puts their house on the market and expects that it will achieve a premium value because it is "special," almost every business owner thinks their business should achieve a multiple of value in excess of the averages being paid today. That's not necessarily a bad position to hold. It shows that you, the owner, takes great pride in what you've achieved over many years of hard work building up the business. That said, in preparation for the sale of your business, it is important to understand the valuation process and have a realistic expectation of the valuation range.

What's realistic? You can secure a typical valuation range from your M&A advisory team (investment banker or broker) if they have an understanding of the idiosyncrasies of your business sector. What do I mean by idiosyncrasies? For instance, a cloud-based software business that has very low *cost of goods sold* will have relatively high EBITDA margins and achieve a high valuation; whereas a cost-intensive manufacturing business with hundreds of employees and lots of inventory and maintenance will have lower EBITDA margins and a lower valuation. That's just due to the vagaries of what it costs to create and deliver your products. It's important for your M&A advisor to possess a demonstrated expertise in the business sector they are representing.

There are databases available to investment bankers and brokers that show the actual valuations of the sale of businesses similar to yours that have been recently sold.

"Strategic buyers" (e.g. your potential competitors) and "financial buyers" (private equity investors) use these same valuation ranges to determine the value of your business. So, having this valuation information is an essential first step in the sale of your business and deciding what is reasonable.

Knowing the *average valuation range* being paid for businesses like yours is a critical initial step, but it represents an *average* and not necessarily what you will get in terms of valuation for your business. Whether you receive offers below, at average, or a premium above the average valuation range will all depend on other factors beyond just the financial performance of your business. Here's a list of some of these factors:

- **Quality of Earnings:** Are your earnings sustainable? Or was a great recent year a "sugar high" of earnings, which is unlikely to repeat?

- **Market Strength at the Time of Sale**: If your business sector is strong, this will have a direct impact on the valuations paid for your business. Other factors that affect valuations are plentiful, including raw material costs, the cost of labor, the cost of healthcare and pension programs, and other items, such as the cost of fuel or interest rates.

- **Strength of the Management Team**: A buyer of your business will very likely want to keep the team in place that made the company as strong as it is today. If you have a strong "bench" of management talent, and they're willing to stay with the company after the sale, that will heighten the value of your business. If you have a leadership team, which is going to vacate as soon as the transaction is complete, that will devalue your business accordingly. Good management and leadership continuity invariably lead to a higher price paid for your company.

- **Market Position and Competitive Landscape**: If your business is in a crowded market and you are fiercely competing for new clients, and/or fiercely competing to keep legacy clients, this will cause a downward pressure on your valuation. A buyer will look at where you are in the competitive landscape and determine your relative strengths against other businesses in your region or those that compete with you. A solid market position, or a dominant presence in a competitive landscape will help you achieve the highest value possible.

- **Product Mix and Services**: A company whose product or services mix is overly concentrated in one area (or with one brand) does not show enough diversity to attract a shrewd buyer. Buyers like to see a balanced mix of products and services to show that the company is diversified, thereby lowering risks. If you have a good mix, it demonstrates that you have managed your company well, and this should be reflected in a high valuation.

- **Customer Concentration**: If you have one customer who accounts for more than 10% of your business, or one customer whose loss would affect earnings in a meaningful and negative way, a buyer will devalue your business accordingly. A diverse customer base is essential to a good valuation.

- **Asset Quality**: The quality of the assets being sold will impact the multiple on your earnings. A company that has driven up its earnings by foregoing maintenance (on building, land, or equipment), shorting inventory, or undermining the strength of its management team with low salaries is not going to be as attractive as a company that takes care of its equipment, its inventory, and its employees.

The M&A Process

A *controlled auction*. Selling your business is a one-time event and one of the most important business decisions that you will make. The execution of the sale of your business must be done with the utmost professionalism if you are to optimize the value of your business. That process typically starts with a M&A advisory firm preparing an *informational memorandum* (IM) also called a *confidential informational memorandum*, (or CIM), that builds a narrative around your business and explains the various financial declarations that are the *central part* of the IM. In addition to presenting your financials, leadership profiles, and competitive landscape (among other aspect of your business), the *informational memorandum* should tell a powerful story about your company, its history, and its culture. Done well, the *informational memorandum* should look more like a brochure than a financial document.

Next Steps:

- As the preparation process is completed and outreach is made to the broadest possible community of buyers, the M&A advisory firm should extract a premium valuation (with acceptable terms and conditions) through a *controlled auction* to a group of serious and pre-qualified buyers. Under this selling scenario, in a process entirely managed by your M&A advisory firm, buyers privately bid against one another for your business, and you decide what is the best offer based on your sales objective.

- Your M&A advisory firm should identify all potential qualified acquirers ("targets") who may have an interest in acquiring your business. It is not unusual for the potential targets to number in the thousands. There are databases that tell which strategic and financials buyers have been active in your sector, and your M&A advisor should have access to these resources.

- In addition to the *informational memorandum*, your M&A advisory firm should prepare a one-page "teaser" that is initially sent to each of the targets. The teaser summarizes your business, and lists recent financial performance without actually naming your business.

- Confidentiality Agreements (CAs) are sent along with the "teaser" by the M&A advisory firm. No IMs should be sent until the CAs are signed.

- Once everything is in place, outreach is made usually via email, and your business goes to market.

Getting Started with the M&A Process

Surrounding yourself with a strong advisory team to manage the sales process is critical to achieving your sales objective and enables you to run your business during the sales process. Here are three key components to getting started:

- An M&A advisory firm (a.k.a. investment banker, "IB," or broker) that really understands the business and the market. It should have the staff to prepare and execute the methodology and steps described above. M&A advisory is not done well by a one or two-person operation.

- A transaction attorney who specializes in M&A transactions and can handle the Letters of Intent and Sales Agreements (a.k.a. *Asset Purchase Agreement, Stock Purchase Agreement,* or *Definitive Purchase Agreement*) once you decide on the winning acquirer.

- An accountant on-call, who can assist with the quality of earnings report and provide the required financial documentation.

There is no more exciting time in the life of the business owner than when he or she can sell a business for meaningful profit after many years of building the business value. The cost of hiring an M&A advisor is a small price to pay to prepare your business for sale, make it as attractive as possible to a potential buyer, maximize the value obtained, and allow you to run your business successfully during the process.

"If you can't explain it simply, you don't understand it well enough."

– Albert Einstein

Chapter 2

Your Business is Worth What Someone Will Pay for It

There is a person I know from our town who has a nice house she needs to sell. She asked me to take a look at it and tell her, just ballpark, what she should list it for.

I walked through the house —*nice place!* — but in a rural setting, far from town. I said it would be a stretch, but that she should list it for $400,000.

"$400,000!?" she shrieked. *"No way!* That's a special house. I have to get $650,000 for the cash I need, and that's what I'm listing it for."

That was three years ago, and it's still on the market, dropping $10,000 each time she changes realtors.

In our mergers and acquisitions practice, that same dynamic occurs when a buyer calls our firm. Early on, we ask, *Have you thought about what you want for the business?* It's not unusual to hear, *Well, I need to get $10 million.*

Then we ask, *How did you arrive at that figure?*

And the seller says, *Well, I need to pull $100,000 a year for my retirement, pay off my bank notes, and settle up with the IRS. I figure I'm going to live another 15 to 20 years. So I need $10 million to make the numbers work.*

Just like the overpriced house, that's a business that may still be on the market three years from now, looking for a buyer who agrees with the $10 million value.

The homeowner and the business owner had a value in their mind before the fair market values were calculated realistically. Like it or not, a house or a business is worth what someone will pay for it, not what the owner needs for retirement.

Your business is your baby. You've invested decades building up the clientele. You've added facilities, capabilities, great staff. Maybe you've weathered (*barely!*) the Great Recession, and survived a few other recessions before that. You've eaten bad debt and skipped a vacation or two so you had enough cash to hand out Christmas bonuses. You're right to expect a reward for your hard work. But that recognition will come through the *performance* of your business, the *quality* of your earnings, and the *sustainability* of the business on a go-forward basis.

What Really Motivates a Buyer?

Typically, a prospective buyer will be motivated initially by the strategic fit of your business, e.g. your product lines, customer mix, and geographical reach. If those requirements are met," the buyer does a financial analysis, which looks at the sales, gross profit margins, OPEX, and EBITDA margin trends over the last three years. They will also want your projections for the coming year. Additionally, the leadership team you have assembled and the workplace culture you have established play an important role in boosting the quality of your earnings, and those contributions should not be minimized.

As for value, in most industries valuations are based on a multiple of adjusted EBITDA. All industries go through cycles. In good markets, high-performing, well-run companies with great cultures will achieve the upper range of valuations; lower-performing ones in the lower range. That's obvious. But when selling your business, we counsel taking a good look at the financials, and—given today's multiples, which are easy to determine—arrive at a realistic value that fully accounts for your earnings and for the intangibles you may bring to the valuation equation. An investment banker's, job is to fight fiercely to maximize that value, and an M&A advisory firm worth its salt *regularly* discovers value-enhancing features and credits to EBITDA that which might be missed by the seller. That said, your expectations should be ultimately tied to your financial statements. That's where your hard work and sacrifice are most-accurately reflected, and will be ultimately rewarded with the highest possible value for your company.

"You miss 100% of the shots you don't take." – Wayne Gretzky

Chapter 3

How Best to Prepare to Go to Market

I used to work with a large building products manufacturing marketing department, and the executive in charge had a saying that's always stuck with me. Whether we were preparing the marketing, packaging, messaging, or trade show presence for product rollouts, he'd say, *Well-presented, half sold.*

That's true for product launches, but it's also true when you are selling your company. The presentation of the company, typically in the form of a deal book—a.k.a. *informational memorandum*— along with accompanying financial statements and tax returns, is viewed as an indicator of the *overall* state of the company and its operations.

Just as you would no more respect a salesman who was sloppy in his communications, late to appointments, or who wasn't dressed properly for a meeting, so too you would hold suspicious a company going to market with haphazard financial statements, or one which had paid no real attention to creating an attractive information-rich informational memorandum.

A prospective client recently asked me, *What's the one thing we should do to prepare for a sale of our company?*

Is it boosting earnings? Sure, that helps. But it's not the #1 item.

Is it to ensure leadership continuity? Essential to have, yes, but not at the top of the list.

Is it paying off debts? Debt-free companies are certainly attractive, but when going to market, there's something even more important, and that's to get your *financial statements* in order so that your balance sheets and profit-and-loss (P&L) statements are clean and presented in standard formats.

What's more, you will need these statements for the last three years along with statements detailing your *trailing twelve months* to be sure to capture good performance even if you are in the middle of a fiscal year. In addition, you will need to prepare projections for the rest of the current year and for the next twelve months.

Presenting these statements in GAAP accounting formats (*general accepted accounting principles*), will make sure that they can be easily read, even by someone who is not familiar with the idiosyncrasies of your company. That way one year can be compared to another, and information made readily available for your investment banker brokering the sale of your company. They will need to calculate year-over-year progress, compounded annual growth rates for revenues, EBITDA, EBITDA margins, and year-to-date performance, all in multiple categories, including gross profit margins, operating expenses, operating income, and bottom line earnings. Clean statements also make it easier to argue for *and defend* adjustments to EBITDA for non-recurring expenses that won't be assumed by the new owner, but which boost the value of your company, sometimes dramatically.

Additional items you will need to have in "pin clean" presentation mode are your inventory statements—knowing that they will be physically redone just before the deal closes—a list of other assets, and your recent tax returns. (More on this later in this book.)

A "One-Page" Approach

Our firm recently worked with a company we took to market, and a prospective buyer wanted to see a list of assets, to understand, as he put it, "everything that would be ours if we wrote you a check today."

Impressively, we had it at-the-ready, in a one-page format. And that's what elicited the following comment from the prospect: "Gosh, it's nice to see everything on one page."

Of course, you can't present every aspect of the company in one-page formats. But a distillation of data in a condensed presentation goes a long way toward assuring this prospective buyer that:

1. The seller knew what the assets were and how much they were worth.

2. That the prospective buyer could trust us to produce, on-demand, summary data and documents that he needed to see when appraising the value of his potential purchase.

Plainly stated, it built trust.

How do you create these clean documents, in formats even strangers can readily understand?

Work with your accounting firm and directly with a CPA. If you are doing the books yourself in a system like QuickBooks, you may find that the statements drawn from in-house use of QuickBooks are not going to be adequate. So, invest the money and the time for an accounting firm to create the genuine articles. Because... *Well-Presented, Half Sold.*

"Luck is the residue of design." – Branch Rickey

Chapter 4

With Markets Strong, Should You Delay Selling?

Let's say your market sector is roaring. Everyone's doing great, and party confetti seems to fall like snowflakes every time you look at your monthly sales reports. Projections indicate that this will continue to be a great year or two for your industry.

Lots of business owners we talk to ask us, "With the markets going so well, why should I sell now? Or should I ride the economy up for a couple more years?"

As much as everyone understands that the worse time to sell a business is during a bad economy, people generally don't hold the reciprocal perception that a strong economy is a great time to sell a business. That's because everything thinks the party will go on forever.

The fact is, most industries are cyclical. Make no mistake, a good market will cycle down, and experience shows that when the music stops, there's not going to be enough chairs for everyone to grab a seat in time.

That's when I tend to get calls from business owners who— emotionally or financially unwilling to endure another recession— will say, "I probably should have called last year, because now I have to wait out another down cycle, or sell for less today." While your business may not be exactly at its peak, it may be wise to start thinking about taking an exit ramp, especially if you are getting older and want to work more on your fishing or golf skills than spend Saturdays with your bookkeeper. There will always be a niggling fear that you left a little money on the table, but... What's that old business cliché? *You've made a smart move if you sold just before the peak.*

Do the Math

Let's take a look at a drop of 2x in valuation (from a 7x to a 5x) due to a faltering economy. And for ease of math, let's say that you were earning $1,000,000 in EBITDA. That drop in multiple means that someone who was going to pay $7,000,000 for your business will now be willing to pay $5,000,000. If you sell at 5x, you would need to increase your EBITDA by 40% just to get back to a *dollar valuation* equal to the 7x multiple of EBITDA you might have obtained in a good market. If your EBITDA is $1 million today, you'd have to generate an EBITDA of $1.4 million *in a down market* at 5x to get the same value for your company you'd get today at 7x with a $1 million EBITDA. I'm sure it goes without saying that increasing EBITDA by 40% in a down market will be nearly impossible.

Given how long it takes to complete a deal—from the *informational memorandum* to the *definitive purchase agreement*— should you sell today, near the peak or risk waiting out another cycle to get a higher value? A *middle path* might be to start preparing now, by obtaining a valuation of your business from an outside advisory firm, and perhaps even testing the market to see whether offers might be forthcoming. You can always say "no," or, if presently surprised by a strong offer, "yes."

"If you don't know where you are going, you might wind up

someplace else."

– Yogi Berra

Chapter 5

Can You "Time the Market" for the Sale of Your Company?

"Timing the market" is something that every investment counselor

advises against for your personal finances, and it's no different for

selling your business. In fact, any prudent mergers and acquisitions

advisor would recommend against trying to time the market. The

reason is simple: The only thing you be can sure about in any

economy is what is going on *right now*. Global events are beyond

our control; a cataclysmic disaster (another 9-11) or natural disaster

(earthquake or flood) can set economies reeling. And that's to say

nothing of the unpredictability of accidents at your business location,

or family emergencies.

So, timing the market for the sale of your business may be a matter of simply *acting now*.

Invariably, the reason business owners wait to sell their business is because they want to grow it to get a higher value. Fair enough, but let's look at a scenario where the market takes a bit of a downturn and see how that would wipe out any incremental growth that you were able to achieve.

In good economies, the multiple of earnings paid for the acquisition of typical businesses is between 5x and 7x EBITDA for a deal that pays all cash-at-close. (Multiples can be much higher if the seller shares some risk with the acquirer, e.g. in multi-year earnouts.) That 5x to 7x range is not something arbitrary. It's obtained from databases that base their information on actual deals completed over the previous 12 months, and year-to-year it's fairly consistent.

No matter what the going multiple is in the year of your sale, a strategic buyer who is acquiring a competitor or complimentary business pays the high end of the c multiple range while financial buyers, such as venture funds, private equity groups, or so-called "family offices" (entities that are managing a family's money) typically pay the low end of the range.

Assuming a 5x - 7x range, what happens to that 7x in a downturn if you don't time your sale correctly? It drops, obviously. If the economy tightens even a little bit, that multiple might move to 6x, 5x, or much lower. What are the implications of this downturn?

As mentioned elsewhere in this book, if your business is worth a 7x EBITDA today, but drops to 5x in a sour market, you would need to increase your EBITDA by a whopping 40% just to get back to a dollar valuation equal to the 7x multiple being used in today's market. If the economy tightens, and you don't want to sell at a 5x or lower, you would have to wait out a multi-year business cycle to see valuations return to what they are today.

In Hindsight, I Wish I'd...

Obviously, you want to sell your business when it is doing well *and* the industry sector is healthy. Just as an unprofitable business has little value in a good economy, a company with historically strong earnings will not achieve its highest value if it is sold when the economy is on the decline or in the tank. Selling today at a 7x, even when you suspect you could achieve a higher value, would likely be a great move in retrospect if the economy were to constrict in the year after a sale.

I can't tell you how often a seller comes to our firm with an unrealistic value expectation in mind. Regardless of market conditions, or what period of the business cycle you offer your company for sale, the first step is to set a realistic price for your company. As an M&A advisory, our firm is always clear *early on* about what we think we can obtain, given current market conditions. If the seller believes we are setting our sights too low, we often recommend that they consider engaging another advisor.

Knowing the price range being paid, *and* having everyone agree on what's reasonable, is a critical early step in the selling process. With that consensus, the seller and the advisory team can work together with confidence and set realistic goals for the sale.

"I failed my way to success." – Thomas Edison

Chapter 6

Acquirers Want Leadership Continuity % Succession Planning

Think of your business as if it were a large tactical ship. Now, imagine a potential acquirer of that ship admiring it from the shore.

"Wow," the fellow says, "look how well that ship runs! The officers in charge manage it perfectly!" Everyone looks up in awe as it sails by. *I've got to buy it!*

Next thing you know, the acquirer makes a successful offer. He can't wait to get aboard and meet the great leadership team and crew, only to be disappointed when he walks onto the bridge to see that all the officers have left.

His first words would be: "Who's going to run this operation? Where's the captain? And where's that great executive officer? I thought I was buying the ship and the entire team!"

This reaction upon finding the ship's empty bridge is no different than you would see from someone who acquired your company only to find out that the leadership had all jumped ship when the transaction closed.

We all know that the leadership of a company—as well as the "crew" they assemble and the culture they establish—are what make a company successful. It's that leadership the acquirer needs to move the company forward, to take advantage of their institutional knowledge and their relationships to employees, the brand, the vendors, and the banks. Acquirers want *leadership continuity*, and if there is no leadership continuity, the acquirers want to see a sophisticated, highly professional process of *succession planning* to guarantee leadership performance through a leadership transition. Without exception, in the absence of leadership continuity or succession planning, acquirers will either walk away, or severely devalue a leaderless or poorly led company.

What the Experts Say

Tony Misura, president of the Misura Group, a leading executive recruitment firm, understands the importance of leadership succession.

If you want the executive succession to be factored into the valuation of the sale, acquirers will want to see the trailing three year's financials, during which the future leaders of the company had significant authority, Tony recently told me.

Naturally, if an acquirer likes those financials, they'll want to keep the leadership that put up those numbers. And if some of that leadership is not going to stay on under new ownership (e.g., when owners cash out), then those leaders have to be replaced by new people that the acquirer believes have the talent to steer the ship in the future.

Tony adds, *Keep in mind that putting a solid team in place can be a three- to four-year process. If you've made the wrong hire in the run-up to the sale of the business, you need enough time to determine if a particular hire was ill-advised. Harvard Business Review reported that Fortune 500 leaders run about 50% success rate on hiring decisions.*

The lesson here is clear: Don't wait until the last minute to install a new team that will remain in place post-acquisition. The leadership should be an integral part of the success of the operation that's being acquired, and they should have been in place for a meaningful period of time—surely enough time to prove that they are the right team to make the operation a continued success. What's more, the leadership team that will remain in place must know about the potential pending sale of the company. You can only imagine the damage control you'd have to do if you suddenly broke the news to the management team that you've sold your company, only to have half of them storm off, resentful that they weren't kept in the loop.

Family Involved?

Ensuring leadership continuity and success planning can have added complications if the business is family-owned and family-run. When multiple family members own different percentages of the company, and some want to leave and some want to stay on, it is probably advisable that an impartial (non-family-member) consultant be involved in constructing the go-forward leadership team *and* that advisor should be vested with some power.

Although granddad and dad might have done a great job building up the company over the decades, junior might not be the executive material that an acquirer wants in place. If a family insists that junior be the new CEO, and the acquirer isn't exactly thrilled with that prospect, the acquirer may devalue the company accordingly or entirely lose interest and walk away.

This is where that dispassionate outsider can step in, preserve the value that is at risk of being lost, and get the right leaders installed. Even with the most structured system in place, it's hard to avoid awkward family conversations. But it's better to have those conversations now, rather than in the heat of the sale of your company.

"Almost all quality improvement comes via simplification..." – Tom Peters

Chapter 7

What Happens to Real Estate When Businesses Are Acquired?

Many businesses I speak with about mergers and acquisitions own the buildings and land where their businesses operate. Sometimes a separate LLC or incorporated business owns the real estate; sometimes it's owned by the business; and sometimes it's owned personally by you, the business owner. In any event, most businesses pay rent to themselves or to their own real estate holding company.

No matter how the real estate is held, most businesses that want to be acquired usually desire to sell the real estate with the business, as part of one clean package.

Only one problem.

Most buyers want to acquire your business for the cash flow. They don't want to invest, say, $1 million or more in real estate that doesn't contribute meaningfully to their earnings. Most will resist "becoming their own landlord."

Who can blame them? Parking that much capital in real estate makes a big portion of their investment, essentially, *dead money*. So, when preparing to sell your business, it usually makes sense to create an LLC or corporation that owns the real estate *separately* from your business operations. In this arrangement, the operation, no matter who owns it, pays rent to the holding corporation. (Many companies already have this arrangement in place.)

Steps to Prepare

If you are preparing to sell your business, before going on the market, work with your investment banker to get the land and buildings appraised. In most cases, even though the acquirer would prefer not to own the land or the buildings, it is prudent to split out the appraised value of your holdings categorically, so you can agree on a reasonable rent.

Get appraisals for fair market *sale value* and fair market *rent value*. With these figures in mind, the corporation that owns the real estate can set lease terms, no matter who pays it. Note that these rent and sale values are often subject to challenge at bargaining time in the acquisition process, so be fair and get substantive multiple opinions to arrive at a current "FMV" (*fair market value*).

How Rent Affects Value

Next, you have to consider how the rent affects the value of your company. Keep in mind that when you sell your business, the rent you have been paying has been charged against the business, so it was an operating expense and it is already "baked into" the EBITDA calculation. (The EBITDA is the figure to which a multiple is applied when determining the value of your business.)

It is important that you are currently charging a FMV rent to the business that can be validated through a FMV rent analysis, through a third party. Under a long-term lease arrangement with the new ownership, they will insist on a FMV rent. If you are charging the business now with higher than FMV rent, it will be adjusted to FMV rent and will be a negative adjustment to EBITDA. If you are charging the business below FMV rent, the new ownership may try to hold that rent and you will be renting to the new ownership *under* FMV rent. To take this issue off the table during negotiations, it is simply best to make sure you are charging FMV rent to the business.

In summary, as much as you would like to just sell the entire operation to a new owner—including the buildings and land—that rarely happens. Most acquirers will want a lease-back, rather than park their capital in real estate where it is not actively generating a return. Finally, note that most M&A advisors will count the dollar value of the lease in the TEV (*total enterprise value*) of the deal, and that lease value will be included in the calculation of the advisor's success fee.

"If you really look closely, most overnight successes took a long time." – Steve Jobs

Chapter 8

Trailing Twelve Months Earnings

Let's say it's October 1st, and you are in the process of selling your company.

Let's also say that your financial statements are prepared on the basis of a calendar year (January 1 to December 31). In other words, you are still three months shy of completing your fiscal year.

Let's also assume that you are having a *killer year* in sales. My goodness, you haven't put up sales numbers in years! Salespeople have a snap in their step; there's a gleam in the eye of the sales VP, and everyone's feeling confident. What's more, since you've taken strong steps to control your costs in recent years, the strong sales figures are contributing to a healthy bottom line. Your company earnings haven't looked this good in years.

Since you are selling your company, the main question on your mind is simple: *Even if we have not completed the current fiscal year, how can we use these strong current earnings in the calculation of our company's valuation? How can we avoid tying our value solely to the last completed fiscal year?*

Your concern is very real, and it can mean the difference between taking home a great sum of money or leaving a pile of it on the table.

To underscore the importance of this issue, let's do some quick math. Let's say that companies like yours are being acquired for multiples of around 7x adjusted EBITDA.

Knowing that multiple, get your calculator and run some numbers. For every $100,000 you add to your EBITDA, you are rewarded with an additional $700,000 in company value at the time you are acquired.

If your EBITDA in the last fiscal year was $1,000,000, and you're acquired for 7x, then the *total enterprise value* (TEV) of your company is $7,000,000.

If you had added $100,000 to the EBITDA, your company value would have been $1,100,000 x 7, or $7,700,000, a very nice lift indeed. In other words, you are essentially getting $7 in increased TEV for every $1 you add to EBITDA.

If it's October, and your current year is not yet complete, you surely have sales projections for the rest of the year. Projections are well and good, but an acquirer will want to see actual EBITDA, on a historical basis; they have only so much faith in projections. After all, investors are naturally cautious. (Who knows what could happen in the remaining months of the year? A weather calamity? Faltering health of a key company owner? A terrorist attack?)

The path to obtaining the valuation boost you deserve for strong ongoing earning is a *trailing twelve months* earnings calculation, also known as "TTM."

By presenting TTM to a potential acquirer, you are essentially showing the results of your last 12 months of performance, but not your last calendar year. Instead, you are showing them EBITDA from, *per se*, a *rolling Fiscal Year* that ends on the last day of every previous month. Very simply put: TTM rewards you for your very latest earnings performance.

As you move deeper into your company's "real" complete year, you should still calculate your TTM after every month, whether you are selling your company or not. Be sure to load in *all* your ongoing costs; don't wait until year-end, because you'll be deceived by phantom earnings.

With the TTM calculation, you also have your finger directly on the pulse of your business. You can detect—practically in *real time*—if the company's earnings are turning sour and need help, or when earnings are going through the roof, confirming that you're on the right track. Waiting to the end of the calendar year to calculate EBITDA doesn't give you much chance for a mid-course fix, unless you've mastered the ability to go back in time, and everyone knows only Michael J. Fox and Doc Brown can do that.

Finally, TTM is a widely accepted metric in the mergers and acquisitions sector, since it reflects your actual performance over the last twelve months. By using TTM, and insisting that you get a multiple of earnings on your current sales, and not those from a year ago, TTM can help you ask for the highest possible value for your business at the time of sale.

"People who succeed have momentum. The more they succeed, the more they want to succeed, and the more they find a way to succeed. Similarly, when someone is failing, the tendency is to get on a downward spiral that can even become a self-fulfilling prophecy." –
Tony Robbins

Chapter 9

What's Your Customer Concentration?

Imagine if you had only one customer. Make no mistake, it would have to be a *big* customer to keep your business busy. But with only one customer, you'd have only one income stream. And you'd be extremely watchful of that customer's purchasing behavior, because your entire business would be dependent on them. Everything that happened to that customer, good or bad, would happen to you.

So, why not spread the risk?

Of course, that's exactly what you do in your business today, by selling to hundreds, if not thousands, of customers each month. By doing so you lower the chances that a loss of any one customer would have a catastrophic effect on your business.

It's important not to have too much revenue financial concentration among your biggest clients, especially if the collapse of just a few of them would mean the failure for your entire company.

The Reveal

If you ever seek an acquirer, the *informational memorandum* that your investment banker produces to take your company to market will have a section that reveals your *Customer Concentration*. It's a crucial and telling section of the *Informational Memorandum*, because every potential acquirer will want to see how much of your business would drop away if you lost a few of your biggest buyers.

Is heavy concentration at the top really a bad thing? Not necessarily, if those top customers are stable and pay on time. You'd probably be surprised to see how many companies have as much as 40% or more of their business concentrated in a dozen customers. In fact, if you're lucky, some large customers can actually be less costly to serve, and it's a benefit to do a great deal of business with them. They often have technology (e.g. mobile portals for managing purchase orders) to smooth out delivery and payment schedules. Plus, your invoicing might be simpler when you are sending a superbill to a national-grade accounting department, with a strong cash position and a seven-figure credit line. High-quality receivables from large buyers can be an asset, not a liability... until there is *too much* concentration in too few accounts.

That might make an acquirer a little nervous, generating a request for more detail about the nature of the customers you are dealing with at that level. (As a rule of thumb: No one customer should represent more than 10% of your business.)

Discounting at the Top

In addition to looking at revenue concentration among your top customers, a potential acquirer will also want to see the gross profit margin (GPM) for *each* of those customers. Their interest in the GPMs is more than just idle curiosity. The acquirer wants to know if you are heavily discounting to your high-volume buyers. If you are, that's a source for some concern, because you may be delivering large volumes of product at very low margins, a scenario that would ding your company valuation.

However, if your GPMs are around the same as the GPMs you are achieving from your other customers, that shows you run a tight ship, and that you've stuck to your guns when negotiating price, even with your high-volume purchasers. That's one sure sign of a well-run business.

If you have not calculated your customer concentration, it would be an instructive exercise to engage in today. Calculate your GPMs for your top customers, and while you are at it, compare those figures to the GPMs of your lowest-revenue customers to see how they stack up by comparison. If you are preparing to sell your company, make adjustments now, as much as you can. Then, when you are finally ready to show your books to a potential acquirer, you'll have the data to readily put their concerns about customer concentration to rest.

"Don't be distracted by criticism. Remember—the only taste of success some people get is to take a bite out of you." – Zig Ziglar

Chapter 10

Maximize Business Value with Credits to EBITDA

EBITDA, a GAAP financial measure, is a key component in the valuation of your business. The reason is simple: EBITDA is used as a proxy for operating cash flow. However, often overlooked in the sale of a business are the adjustments you can make to your earnings, a.k.a. *Adjusted EBITDA* (a Non-GAAP financial measure) that can have a significant impact on business valuation.

For example, a typical valuation multiple is 7x EBITDA, so a company booking $3million in EBITDA would sell for $21 million. But let's say you found $300,000 to credit to your *Adjusted EBITDA*. That would boost the business value by $2.1 million dollars. So, it's worth taking a good long look at possible credits.

Keep in mind that credits to EBITDA are typically one-time expenses that occur during your fiscal year (or calendar financial accounting year) and which *won't repeat* in the future or after the sale of your business.

As a rule, buyers will closely scrutinize each adjustment to EBITDA, so credits must be legitimate and agreed upon with the buyer. (A word of caution: Don't nickel and dime the adjustments. Adjustments to EBITDA of less than $1,000 should probably not be considered; they are often called "ash and trash.")

To determine what adjustments are typical, consult with your investment banker about what constitutes an adjustment to EBITDA, but here are some typical examples:

- **Owner salaries and bonuses**

As an owner, if your salary plus bonus is $300,000 per year, but the market rate to replace you is $200,000, you can most likely take a legitimate $100,000 adjustment to EBITDA. (Remember the economic value of a $100,000 adjustment is a $700,000 increase in company value!)

- **Rent of the facilities**

If the rent you are charging your business is below fair market value, the difference could be a negative adjustment to EBITDA. If the rent is above fair market value, that would be a positive adjustment to EBITDA, in favor of the buyer. It all depends on the terms of the lease.

- **Personal Owner Expenses**

For private businesses, it's common (though not recommended by the IRS) for some owner's personal expenses to be credited to the business, e.g. a family member that is on the payroll, club memberships, or sports tickets that the acquirer would not pay post-acquisition. Those are likely EBITDA credits.

- **Non-recurring professional fees**

Valid credits to EBITDA include *one-time* legal fees or a settlement from a lawsuit, non-recurring consulting fees, and non-repeating marketing expenses that are attached to a specific marketing program.

- **Infrastructure, equipment, software, IT upgrade investments**

The key to recognizing these credits rests on whether the investment was expensed or capitalized, as opposed to a one-time expense. If it was expensed as a one-time expense, it may be eligible as an adjustment to EBITDA. If it was capitalized, then it is not eligible since it is on a depreciation schedule, which flows through your income statement. Keep in mind you are already getting credit for your depreciation since EBITDA is earnings before interest, taxes, *depreciation*, and amortization. So, one-time expenses, if they are being amortized, would not qualify as an adjustment to EBITDA.

- **Other one-time expenses**

A note of caution: If your one-time expenses have recurred on your income statements in prior years and are projected to show up in future years, they are simply not one-time expenses that can be used as adjustments to EBITDA.

Legitimate expenses vs. non-legitimate one-time expenses that can be used as an adjustment to EBITDA will be readily determined in discussion with your investment banker and your accountant. Be sure to have that discussion so that you don't leave money on the table. Adjustments to EBITDA are common, and it is an opportunity to increase the value of your business, sometimes dramatically. But it needs to be done carefully with one thought in mind: Will the buyer accept the adjustment to EBITDA as legitimate and fair?

"Always look for the fool in the deal. If you don't find one, it's you."

— *Mark Cuban*

Chapter 11

What are Earnouts, and How Do They Work?

An "earnout" is commonly used in merger and acquisitions transactions. Essentially, an earnout is a risk-allocation provision, where part of the purchase price of a company is deferred. The earnout is paid based on the performance of the acquired business over a specific period of time.

The reason earnouts are used is simple: They can bridge the gap between the seller, who wants the highest possible valuation, and the buyer, who may be willing to pay top dollar, but only if the business achieves a specified performance metrics usually based on gross revenue, sales revenue, net profit, or EBITDA, usually based on gross revenue, sales revenue, net profit, or EBITDA.

As discussed elsewhere in this book, when valuing a business, most buyers use data from the last fiscal year, while also examining financial statements that reach back three years or more. But what if the seller is well into the financial year at the time of sale, and he's putting up great numbers, with strong growth? The seller rightfully wants to get rewarded for that performance, which may not be reflected in the last fiscal year's financial reports. In this case, if the seller requests it, the buyers could consider pegging the company's value to the trailing twelve months (TTM) performance, which represents the last twelve months of results prior to the closing.

Ok, let's look at an example. Let's say that a seller wants to sell his business in the middle of the fiscal year. But, with sales on an upswing, he wants a valuation credit for the remainder of the budgeted year. Let's assume this business did $2 million in EBITDA the previous year, and is projected to do $2.3 million in EBITDA in the current year.

Based on a 7x multiple of EBITDA for both periods, the valuation for the previous year's performance would be $14 million. Now, apply the same multiple to the current year, and the valuation rises to $16.1 million. In this scenario, the buyer agrees to the valuation of $14 million based on the previous year's results. The seller is paid $14 million in cash at closing. But the seller doesn't want to leave any money on the table, since he's having a good year. So, for the current year, the buyer and seller agree to a $2.1 million earnout. The earnout will be paid *if* the seller achieves $2.3 million in EBITDA for current year.

When structuring the performance metrics for an earnout, be exceedingly careful and seek advice from an experienced investment banker. As a seller, you want to use fair financial metrics that you can achieve and be able to manage operations you still control after the initial deal has closed. The buyer is typically interested in one financial target: the bottom line, either net income or EBITDA. No matter what metrics are chosen to peg to the earnout, what's really important is that the terms are fully and easily understood, and are perceived as fair by both sides.

Let's look at the seller and the buyer's perspective: The seller needs to be clear about what the buyer will control, *post close*. At a minimum, the seller will want to protect the resources necessary to achieve his earnout targets. But if the buyer is going to tack on additional costs to the seller's business, such as expenses for selling, or general and administrative (SG&A) expenses, then the seller should probably avoid pegging the earnout to EBITDA.

When determining targets for that scenario, consider tying the earnout to sales or gross profit dollars instead of EBITDA. If the buyer agrees that no additional SG&A costs will be added to the business—post close and during the earnout period—then EBITDA can be considered. In any event, a clear understanding of the terms and metrics is essential to keep both sides happy, cooperative, and working together toward their mutual success.

"It's hard to do a really good job on anything you don't think about

in the shower." —Paul Graham

Chapter 12

Earnings Quality: It's the Prospective Buyer's Right to Know

Everyone wants to sell their business at peak earnings. Who

wouldn't? Since most businesses are purchased as a multiple of

earnings, you as a seller have substantial motivation to get those

earnings as high as possible (on a trailing-12-month basis or

previous-fiscal-year/calendar-year basis) before you put your

company up for sale. Every dollar added to EBITDA can bring back

a substantial return in valuation, often 5X, 6X, or even 7X.

Most prospective buyers expect to see this pattern of selling on

an uptick. It's only natural; indeed, any business that tries to sell at a

low point in the business cycle would be looked upon with

suspicion, and accordingly, it would receive a poor valuation.

But buyers considering purchasing companies, which are selling at a time of peak earnings have the right to question two things: the *quality* of those earnings and the *sustainability* of those earnings in the future.

Quality of the Earnings

The quality of the earnings is an indication of how likely they are to continue. High-quality earnings don't necessarily have to show up on your books as repeat business, although that is certainly desirable, since repeat business costs the least to acquire.

But high-quality can also mean consistent earning levels or consistent rates of increases year to year, whether the source is repeat business or new business. High-quality earnings point to a quality sales staff and a disciplined company that works hard to take care of its customers.

Let's look at an example. Say a business shows sales of $25 million three years ago, $27 million two years ago, $29 million last year, and a prediction of $31 million this year. Let's also say that the company has consistently shown 10% EBITDA margins, with an unadjusted EBITDA of $2.5MM, $2.7MM, and $2.9MM respectively, and a projected $3.1MM this year.

A prospective buyer looking at that company will have no problem believing the current fiscal year's projections, even with just a few months of data to go on, because the earnings have shown consistent high-quality growth.

If another business were to show jagged sales and EBITDA margins that bounce around year for year, with no symmetry, followed by a killer year of strong sales and high EBITDA margins, the potential buyer isn't going to have a great deal of faith in a recent, spectacular 12-month period. That's because the recent numbers may not represent a trend that will continue. In fact, they are likely to represent a "sugar high" that can't be consistently replicated. Red flags will pop up on the deal, and valuation won't be based in the trailing twelve months, but perhaps on earnings *averaged out* over the past three years.

Sustainability of Earnings

Simply put, the sustainability of earnings indicates the likelihood that current earnings will continue to grow / keep pace at roughly the same rate as the *cost of goods sold* (COGS) expenditure levels.

It's even more impressive if you can show that you can sustain or increase your earnings while *lowering* COGS over time, indicating that you are always working to drive up efficiency.

If you had a great year, but you know in your heart that you will have to increase marketing costs and salesforce salaries the following year to retain those customers, then the sustainability of the earnings is lower, and your customer retention may be more volatile than current earnings indicate.

The same principle holds for a seller who positions his/her company for sale by making an effort to suppress COGS. Some examples include: deferring necessary maintenance, not filling a position that needs to be filled, or misallocating expenses into a different time period than the allocation of earnings, just to obtain an earnings credit that really should be an expense.

A prudent buyer will examine your COGS along with your maintenance schedules, and historical staffing levels / future staffing needs to see how they have changed over time with respect to your earnings.

Finally, if you reported earnings that you have yet to collect, (e.g. pending AR) and you are using an accrual accounting basis, you will have credited those to EBITDA. But the prospective buyer will be within his/her rights to question whether those reflect accurate earnings, especially if there is a history of bad pays that have not properly been accounted for in your bad debt allowances.

No Tricks

There is no trick to reporting the quality and sustainability of earnings. It's about divulging what's fair and reasonable, properly allocating earnings and expenses, and forthrightly calculating COGS in a way that buyer and seller agree is accurate.

"Perfection is not attainable, but if we chase perfection we can catch excellence." – Vince Lombardi

Chapter 13

The (Irksome) Due Diligence Process

The excitement of receiving a *letter of intent* (LOI) for your business is something all sellers look forward to. The LOI maps out the price a buyer will pay, the terms and timing of the payment, and—if your investment banker has done a good job—early important specifics, such as how the working capital PEG will be calculated. When the LOI is finally negotiated, agreed to, and signed by all parties, the due diligence process begins. The due diligence process is designed to give the buyer a chance to:

1. Verify everything that was stated in the *Informational Memorandum.*

2. Process a long list of clearances and legal issues that need to be resolved before the sale can move to close.

Make no mistake, the due diligence process is time-consuming, and it often distracts the most important people in the business with the chores of information retrieval and financial reporting. Before I get into a sampling of what the due diligence process entails, keep this in mind: This time-consuming nature of the process presents a unique problem for the seller. Here's why. The due diligence process can take upwards of three to four months for a "mid-market" deal. During that time, your company has to hit the financial performance that was predicted in the *Informational Memorandum*. If you miss those numbers, the buyer has the right to reexamine the deal and potentially "re-price" their offer based on the new numbers. (The buyers will almost never go higher if you beat your predictions, but they often go lower if you miss them.)

Unfortunately, the people needed to make those numbers are often the very people distracted by the due diligence process. So, time management and multi-tasking are the watchwords of success here. This is especially true for the CEO, COO, and the CFO (as well as the bookkeepers and your accounting firm).

When the due diligence list comes over from the buyer, be sure you're *sitting down* when you open it. This will lower your risk of injury when you faint. The list is often *a dozen or more pages long*, and can have 200 line items for your team to address. Each line item is a request for information. Here's a sample look at the level of detail that is often required in the due diligence process.

- **HR and Benefits**

A full accounting of every employee's earnings, commissions, bonuses, last raises, and benefits (including 401k plans, and raise / bonus policies), including their hire dates and duration of employment.

- **IT**

All software licenses will need to be current, at your expense; descriptions of security, backup, disaster recovery, and extra capacity plans for databases, as well as all vendor contacts.

- **Security**

"Anyone who touches money" will be subject to a thorough background check, and required to sign a waiver allowing the research to be done.

- **Safety**

Many buyers acquiring a workplace, such as a distribution center,

warehouse, or lumberyard, may be implementing new safety

protocols, and may want to test all employees for, say, hearing, to

establish a baseline that limits their liability down the road.

- **Customer interviews**

All buyers will want to interview a sampling of customers. Requests

for 100 names are not unusual.

- **Site visits and environmental inspection**

Got a toxic spill on your site? A buried tank? Asbestos? This part of

the process will ferret all of that out, typically using an

Environmental Site Assessment (ESA) test.

I've listed just six possibilities of what might be 200 request

categories. And I haven't even gotten into the financial reporting

required, e.g. trial balances, balance sheets and P&L by division (all

to be supplied *each month* during due diligence), receivables aging, inventory and inventory reserve balances, etc. The list really does go on and on.

Ready to handle that, as you run a successful business?

The companies that handle this process well are the ones that exclusively charge an employee or two with the task of rounding up the material and dogging the information and data. You can't complete the process by paying attention to it for a few minutes each day.

Dropbox is a superb tool for managing the process. Secure access can be granted to multiple parties, and folders and sub-folders can be set up for each line item, so compliance can be readily checked. Email alerts can let all parties know every time a file is added or edited. Also, with Dropbox, you won't be emailing files and wrestling with version control as information is edited and updated.

The relief felt when the due diligence process is completed is *almost* better than the thrill of seeing funds wired to you at closing. *Almost.*

"If one does not know to which port one is sailing, no wind is favorable." — *Lucius Annaeus Seneca*

Chapter 14

Are You Too Ready to Sell?

We often get inquiries from business owners who start the conversation this way: "Well," (deep sigh of relief) "I'm finally ready to sell."

But all too often, they are too ready to sell. That's because the owner has decided not just to sell, but to fully retire as soon as possible, with no intentions to stay on to manage the business post-acquisition. That owner wants to hand over the keys, take the check to the bank, and maybe work on his or her sailing skills.

Unfortunately, as attractive as it may be for an owner to dust off their hands and walk away, that quick exit is highly frowned upon by acquiring companies. Worse, it can cost the departing owner millions of dollars in lost valuation.

Here's why: Most acquiring companies want business continuity. They want to keep the leader (indeed, the whole team) in place that made the company so successful. Most acquiring companies want at least a year of post-acquisition service from the departing owner, ideally more.

If the owner says they're "out the door," that can easily knock the price of a company down a "turn" or two (2x), if not more. In other words, if the company would have been purchased at a 6x multiple of EBITDA, the deal might sink to 5x EBITDA. If the EBITDA is $1,000,000, the company won't sell for $6,000,000, but for $5,000,000 instead.

Here's another way to look at it: If the departing owner were told that he'd be given $1,000,000 to stay an additional year, he'd probably jump at the chance, because, well, that's a lot of juice. Yet when that same departing owner insists on leaving the company immediately upon an acquisition, he may not have the perspective to see how much money he is leaving on the table with a lower valuation.

Prepare with Replacement Personnel

If you are an owner, and you want to leave as soon as your company is acquired, why not take the prudent step of replacing yourself a year in advance of the sale?

That takes some real patience and planning; make no mistake. But the planning ahead may prevent an owner from making an impulse call to an investment banker to say, "I'm finally ready to sell." Plus, as an added benefit to the valuation equation, the departing owner's salary, benefits, and related costs can often be credited to the EBITDA, since it is not going to be a recurring future cost.

Now, how do you install a replacement for yourself? No matter what your title— president, CEO, or COO —if you can't promote talent from within, bring in a top-notch executive recruiter, and get your replacement installed at least 12 months before you pull the trigger on a sale.

When searching for your replacement, be completely transparent about your plans. Inform the incoming executive that he or she is there to take over in a transition that includes a planned change of ownership. (Note that acquiring companies often put incentives and equity in place for senior executives as a retention strategy, which can be a bonus for the incoming talent.) An ambitious replacement executive will see a real chance to prove his worth, and he or she can have a year ramp-up to make his mark.

With the replacement in place, the outgoing owner can ease out of operations and serve as a senior advisor, a role he or she may want to continue to play in the year(s) after an acquisition as well. As for the acquiring company, it will likely not view the departure of the owner as a high-impact loss, because so much preparation has been made to replace his or her talents and fill the roles he or she played.

Finally, this preparation "pays well." With the right executive in place, and the outgoing owner's transition so well managed, think of how much company value will have been protected and preserved. It is far more than the all-in costs of the new hire, to say nothing of what this leadership continuity does to ensure a smooth transition of ownership for all of the employees.

"The secret to success is to know something nobody else knows." —
Aristotle Onassis

Chapter 15

Asset Sale or Stock Sale?

One common question that comes up as a deal moves toward a
closing is whether the sale should be an asset sale or a stock sale.

A couple of quick points before we get into specifics: First, this
chapter contains around 1/100th the information required to
adequately cover this topic. So, any decision you make— asset vs.
stock— must be made in consultation with your accountant and tax
attorney. Second, in the "lower middle market" (up to $100 million
in sales), 70%+ of sales are asset sales, because, to put it bluntly,
that's what buyers demand.

Of the five different company types, (sole proprietorships,
LLCs, partnerships, C-corporations and sub-S corporations), each
has idiosyncrasies that will affect your election. However, "non-

corporate entities" (sole proprietorships, LLCs, and partnerships) can present a special tax peril for the sellers, and no one-size-fits-all rule applies. In the most general terms, the election to go with an asset sale or a stock sale largely depends on the legal liability assumed by the acquirer, and by the tax implications to the seller and acquirer.

Liabilities. In an asset sale, the acquirer gets to rule in and rule out what assets it wants to purchase, whereas in a stock sale the liabilities are not just the encumbrances of the assets, but also any liability that may arise for wrongdoing of the entity under its prior ownership... unless the seller rules out certain liabilities in the "representations and warranties" within the purchase agreement.

(See why most acquirers want an asset sale?)

Depreciation. In an asset sale, the acquirer's basis for depreciation is the fair value paid for each asset, or class of assets, regardless of the tax basis of each asset or all assets taken aggregately. To the extent that the fair value of the company is greater than the fair value of its assets, this "excess" is allocated to "goodwill," which is depreciated for tax purposes as a separate asset over 15 years. So, the acquirer has an incentive to allocate as much of the purchase price as possible to assets with the shortest recovery periods, determined with reference to the allocable purchase price. The seller's gain is determined with reference to the basis in each asset sold rather than the aggregate basis of all assets.

(Again, you see why acquirers want an asset sale.)

Rights: In a stock sale, there may be a risk of minority stock holders blocking a sale. Many corporations protect minority shareholder rights by agreement, but such agreements can also compel minority shareholders to sell their interests, even when they don't agree with the majority. This a frequent occurrence. (Minority shareholders may also assert their rights by filing a lawsuit claiming that majority shareholders are betraying fiduciary duties.)

Assets. Note that in an asset sale, there are some assets that are difficult for a seller to assign to an acquirer, such as a rail siding agreement, or a land-use covenant assigned to the seller's family; licenses, permits… the list goes on. A stock sale entitles the acquirer to these assets without a reassignment, driving down legal costs and the time it takes to close a deal.

Taxes. Generally, the taxes are higher for the seller in an asset sale because of the differential tax rates that may apply to certain types of assets. The seller may end up paying capital gains rate on some aspects of the sale, and the seller's marginal rate on others.

Note that the seller's tax treatment is due to tax rates on certain types

of assets, but also due to exposure to ordinary income treatment for

the portion of gain attributable to recapture of prior depreciation.

What's Right for You?

Confused? I don't blame you. When I'm asked if a stock sale or an

asset sale is preferred, I say, "well, it depends, but the best advice I

can offer is to speak with your tax accountant and a solid tax

attorney."

Every business is idiosyncratic. When determining what's best, we

look at tax implications, the number of share-holders, and how

willing they all are to sell their shares. We also look at the

company's locations, as well as the nature of the assets themselves

(e.g. are there an abundance of licenses, permits, leases, etc.?), and

all potential liabilities – the known knowns and unknown unknowns.

Only then do we make a recommendation that's right for our client.

"If you are willing to do more than you are paid to do, eventually you will be paid to do more than you do." – Anonymous

Chapter 16

Leave Profanity and Politics at the Door

Deals go south and suitors bow out of contention for lots of reasons, typically lack of strategic fit, inadequate cash flow, or because the deal is offered at the wrong time in the business cycle.

Or at least that's what departing suitors will say are the reasons for backing away. But it is surprisingly common for a suitor to back away from a deal because of a cultural or personality mismatch between the buyer and the seller.

On more than a few deals we've been involved in, a promising suitor indicated they were flying in for a big meeting, that the deal looked perfect, and they couldn't wait to meet the ownership team. But after the meeting, their interest cooled immediately.

What gives? They may have been turned off by the personalities of the owners.

Politics. In more than a few cases, even after we'd cautioned our clients to avoid controversial topics, politics get brought up for discussion. That's a big no, no.

You can't predict the politics of the suitor, so don't make an assumption that they will agree with your pronouncements. If the suitor disagrees with your politics, they probably won't mention it initially, out of politeness. But I guarantee you, as soon as they close the car door on the way to the airport, they may very well dismiss the deal as impossible due to a potential mismatch of values. Even if they happen to agree with you, your politics will have little bearing on the value of your company. So why risk bringing it up? It's universally safe to keep political discussions out of the mergers and acquisitions process.

Profanity. I've worked on dozens of construction sites as a young man, so salty language is nothing new to me. And I'm not naïve. I recognize that people who work together over a long period of time can probably let a profane word slip now and again without unduly offending those around them. But that all changes when strangers meet, especially when they meet for the first time.

You cannot assume that it's appropriate to speak profanely in front of people you meet in the deal-vetting process. You simply can't predict how they will respond.

In my decades in business, I have never seen anyone smile or give an encouraging look when someone they've just met speaks profanely. That said, many times I have heard people, as they walk away from a meeting, say, "I have to say, I'm just not comfortable with that language. Can you imagine if they were speaking that way around our offices?"

Whether you're an altar boy or a sailor, zip that lip when you're tempted to spout off with bad language during meet and greets, and in every meeting thereafter.

Libations. Business dinners almost invariably involve a cocktail or a nice bottle of wine, but—especially on the "first date" between a suitor and a seller—a light drink is probably more than enough to put people at ease and open up for some bonding conversations.

Any excess drinking during meet-and-greets is universally looked upon as a negative in a business deal. Even the perception of excess drinking is a no no… Your nightly standard 3rd glass of wine may seem to a suitor as flat-out excess.

Most suitors will likely observe a seller's excesses around libations and think, "I'm just not doing a business deal with a person who drinks like that, especially when they drink like that around someone they are meeting for the first time. How much do they drink around friends, if they drink like that around strangers!?"

Save the all-night toasts for when the deal is done, and you're just among old friends.

Sports. Unless you can all agree to the unspoken truth that Tom Brady is the best quarterback that has ever played football (because, you must admit, he is), it's best to avoid sports, at first. Sports can be a great bonding experience with a stranger, but feel them out first before making blanket pronouncements like the one I just made about the great Tom Brady.

Religion and Ethnic Identification. Here's another area where it's surprised me more than once when a seller makes a comment about a religious or ethnic group. Not only will a suitor's antenna go up around potential discrimination lawsuits and other liabilities, but it's just bad form to imply that you focus on cultural differences inspired by religious or ethnic groups. Keep those discussions to yourself.

Is everyone a perfect gentleman or lady? No, and I'm the first to admit to imperfections. But the topics listed above are ones where you should steer clear of controversy, lest you bring about judgement by someone who might otherwise be willing to write you a big fat check.

"If you can't feed a team with two pizzas, it's too large." — Jeff Bezos

Chapter 17

How Investment Bankers Get Paid for Brokering Sale of Your Business

Investment bankers that broker the sale of your company have a fairly standard schedule for retainers and success fees. But there are idiosyncrasies and potential pitfalls to watch for. So, let's take a close look.

The Retainer: Most investment bankers charge a retainer to prepare your company for sale, often around $50,000. The retainer pays for ongoing expenses to prepare the "deal book" a.k.a. *informational memorandum or "IM"*, which is used to shop the deal to acquirers. But the retainer should be paid out monthly (e.g. $10,000/month), not all upfront.

In many cases the entire retainer is *refunded* to you, the seller, in the event of a success transaction. If the success fee turns out to be $250,000, the first $50,000 is refunded to you when the deal closes. Beware of any investment bank that asks for the entire retainer in advance. After paying it all out, you might find it hard to get the investment banker's attention in three or four months, especially for relatively small deals, e.g. under $10 million.

The retainer pays the investment banker for the substantial hours his staff puts into creating the IM, as well as subscription fees to the expensive databases that are used to develop target lists and obtain the very latest deal values for similar companies that have been recently sold.

Investment bankers will insist on a retainer not only to defray preparation costs, but to make sure sellers have "skin in the game." That way, a seller won't just cavalierly commission an IM (often 40+ pages of company background, with complete financial analysis) only to take the IM and walk away, or represent the company themselves using the investment banker's work.

The Success Fee: In addition to the retainer, most investment bankers charge a success fee based on the percentage of the deal value. A 5% fee is typical.

Some sellers will also ask for a cap on the cash value of the fee, which might make the fee valued at less than 5% of the overall deal value. The capped fee amount depends on the total paid for the company, and it's more likely for an investment banker to agree to a cap if the deal size is substantially over $10 million in value. In that case a cap on the success fee of $500,000 or $600,000 might be viewed as reasonable. But note that the success fee can also be staged, paying 5% of the first $10 million, and then a smaller percentage for between $10 and $20 million, etc. It's all negotiable. If the proceeds of a sale are paid out over time (an *earnout*), the success fee should be paid as you, the seller, are paid over time.

Beware the investment banker who asks for a "guaranteed success fee," no matter the deal size. A guaranteed success fee is often requested for smaller deals, with transaction values under $5 million. If an investment banker seeks a guaranteed $400,000 fee on a deal worth about $4 million, he's really asking for a 10% success fee, twice what he would normally receive. A customer-focused investment banker will typically not ask for a guaranteed fee and is happy to share the risk of the sale with his client.

Is the Success Fee Worth It?

In most deals (and this has invariably been the case with our firm), the investment banker earns back more than his success fee *just with credits to EBITDA,* which the clients would have otherwise missed. In other words, in the investment banker's financial analysis, he finds non-recurring charges, inventory credits, working capital credits, or charges that can be credited under new ownership which, when multiplied by today's valuation multiples (e.g. between 5x and 7x), *more than* earn back what the seller pays in success fees. In that case, the seller is effectively accessing the full range of the investment banker's services at low-cost / no-cost, including the informational memorandum, financial analysis, deal valuation, management of the auction / letter-of-intent processes, as well assistance in drafting the definitive purchase agreement, reps and warranties, asset declaration, and closing processes, to say nothing of help through due diligence.

Although many companies balk at the 5% fee, make no mistake: Investment bankers offer a service that avoids common seller errors, maximizes the sale value of your company, avoids pitfalls, and perhaps most importantly, allows a seller to run his business without distraction (and without the *substantial* demands on his time) from the complicated acquisition process.

"Don't worry about people stealing your design work. Worry about the day they stop." — *Jeffrey Zeldman*

Chapter 18

Top Five Concerns of Sellers & Buyers

I recently moderated a mergers and acquisition panel at a national conference. On the panel, there were two panelists from publically held companies, and two from private equity groups ("PEGs"). No matter where panelists were from, there was a lot of agreement when they responded to questions and concerns discussed with the audience. Here are some highlights:

Real estate: Many businesses want to sell their real estate along with their businesses. But acquirers aren't really interested in your real estate. They are buying your business for the relationships and leadership you have put in place to generate cash flow and profitability. Sellers who stick to the notion that the real estate has to be part of the deal will find the deal stalled, and perhaps DOA.

Start the process of preparing for acquisition by setting up a corporation to hold the real estate and lease to back to the acquirer.

Leadership: Leadership continuity is key to maximizing the value of your business. Don't put your business on the market and boldly announce that all the top executives are leaving. That approach will devalue your company, if you can even sell it. It's important to work back a year or more to install leadership that will stay in place after the acquirer takes over.

Clear up inventory: One M&A panelist gave some great advice about cleaning up inventory before seeking an acquirer: "Don't expect to be paid for old, stale, or slow-moving items sitting in your yards." Beyond cleaning out old inventory, make sure you have digital systems to track and manage inventory. An acquirer will do a physical inventory during their due diligence, but demonstrating control over your inventory is a key to demonstrating you have control over your overall business.

Clear Up AR: If you have AR that is dated, it will reflect poorly on you, even though dated AR is the fault of the borrower and not you. No matter the reason, you'd be well-advised to clean it up and have most accounts sub-30-days net when you take the company to market.

HR: If your business is a family business, and you've been loosy-goosy with HR policies (e.g. verbal employment contract, verbal promises of bonus, no formal harassment policies), get these formalized. If you're running a tight ship that won't require the acquirer to spend time and money to fix, it reflects well on you, and your value.

Working Capital Ratio: This is a complicated matter; so, please see my longer treatment of this topic elsewhere in this book. It used to be that a typical working capital ratio (WCR) was 1.5/1 of assets to liabilities, e.g. $1.50 on hand for every $1 in liability. Although that 1.5/1 is a good baseline, buyers' expectations are constantly changing, and the WCR is negotiated on a case-by-case basis, so that the business has ample cash for operations.

Earnouts. An "earnout" is used as a risk-allocation vehicle, where part of the purchase price of a company is deferred. The earnout is paid based on your performance over a specific period of time, and it's tied to metrics such as gross revenue, sales revenue, or EBITDA. Most of the M&A panelists don't use earnouts when acquiring businesses. This is the case because earnouts are hard to control, especially when an acquired business is co-mingled with a larger enterprise. The large enterprise might take over buying or payroll, and it's difficult to see just who or what contributed to overall performance. Plus, the seller loses control of other aspects of his or her business, such as marketing and hiring of salespeople, further clouding the waters. Most buyers said they'd rather just pay cash at close, and that's the end of the deal.

These were the top concerns of and the panelists speaking to them, but it strikes me that these are universal concerns.

At the end of the day, the common concern is that sellers want a fair price, after putting their company in the best light, yet a buyer's main concern is overpaying. The natural tension between these two dynamics is what drives the deal and the company value. I've found that the best transaction is described by a common cliché: *It's a great deal with the seller thinks they sold it for a little less than it was worth, and the buyer thinks that paid a little more than they should have.*

"Chains of habit are too light to be felt, until they are too heavy to be broken." —*Warren Buffett*

Chapter 19

Can Your Company be Re-Priced After the LOI?

Here's a dreadful prospect that you want to avoid. Let's say that you put your company on the market, and – for ease of math – you are putting up good numbers at the time of sale, say, $2 million in EBITDA.

Your investment banker (broker) sends the deal teaser out to prospects, you get some interested parties, and someone comes in with a Letter of Intent (LOI) that offers a nice price. Say they offer today's going multiple of 5.5X adjusted EBITDA. In this case, the offer would be $11 million.

You like the price, so you turn away the other suitors, and agree to enter into the due diligence process and move toward a closing.

The Letter of Intent will often have a clause in the document that cites your projections for the amount of EBITDA you expect to book between the acceptance of the Letter of Intent and the closing date. To maintain that $2 million EBITDA pace, you have to continue to put around $183,000 in EBITDA each month on the bottom line.

Now what? Well, unfortunately, the due diligence process takes months. During that time, you're substantially distracted (as I've written about before) with a boatload of requests for information, information that you never dreamed someone would ever want to know, e.g. environment assessment of your various real estate locations, drug tests for your truck drivers, introductions to customers to interview...the list goes on and on. In fact, you're so distracted by the due diligence process that you miss your numbers, and you don't earn $183,000 in EBITDA two months before closing. In fact, you miss your number by $20,000. Then, the month before closing, you miss your numbers again, slipping $25,000 below the $183,000 projection.

These slippages off the pace of EBITDA are all reported to the prospective buyer on a monthly basis. That first month you miss your numbers, the buyers may have a few raised eyebrows, and they might even voice some mild concern. But that second month that you slip off the pace is trouble. The buyer may look at the two months as a trend, a downward trend... And they will surely vocalize their concern. The call starts out friendly, and goes something like this:

"Joe, I can't help but notice that you are not making your numbers. Any reason for that? I have to say that we are having some concerns..."

Joe says, "Well, heck Bob, I've been so distracted by all of your requests that I have not had time to focus on managing my sales team. Plus, I have not been able to make the calls that I typically make each month for our biggest customers."

Bob says, "Is your business so unstable and your profits so fragile that a few hours of your time each week can cause the business to tank? I think we have to reprice the deal."

Reprice the deal? That is a phrase that has sent many a seller to the medicine cabinet, scrambling for his heart pills, following by an equally concerned investment banker who is trying to find out exactly how serious the buyer is about repricing.

Now let's look at a couple more points before we look at the math of how a buyer would reprice.

During due diligence, the acquirer will spend a lot of time with management understanding the relationship the target company has with its customers. The acquirer will look at the likelihood that customers will continue to buy through the company, post-close. At the last stage of the due diligence process, the acquirer will speak with the key customers or do a 3rd party satisfaction survey about the company. If the acquirer ascertains through these customer calls and surveys that some customers could be at risk post-close, repricing the deal could come into play.

Finally, even if the company is hitting its sales and EBITDA targets during the due diligence process, if customers are lost during process, it can materially impact the performance of the company of a go-forward basis, and here too, repricing could come into the picture.

Now let's take a look at the math of repricing, which is simple and rather brutal. Since the acquirer is paying on a multiple of EBITDA (e.g., 5.5X), they will apply that same multiple to the new EBITDA, adjusted downward, and calculated over a 12-month period. The $2 million EBITDA that got you an $11 million valuation may drop to $1.7 million, dropping the purchase price from $11 million to $9.35 million. (Remember, every dollar you drop in EBITDA can have a negative implication, X 5.5.)

Ironically, if you exceed your projected numbers during the due diligence process, there is little chance the buyer will reprice upwards, to give you a higher valuation. But negative repricing is all too real.

The ultimate solution: Avoid distractions during the due diligence process; don't neglect sales and bring on staff that you can delegate parts of the due diligence process to. There's nothing worse that working a lifetime to prepare your business for sale, only to have a couple of months of bad performance knock a million dollars or more off your value.

"Whether you think you can, or you think you can't — you're right."

– Henry Ford

Chapter 20

Taming Unrealistic Valuation Expectations

Here's something that's remarkably consistent in merger and acquisitions work: When selling at a time of strong growth, many business owners do not want the valuation of their businesses pegged to where they are *now* with financial performance. They want the valuation based on *future* performance, as yet not achieved. They want a buyer to reward them with a higher contemporary valuation for the *prospects* of growth.

And here's another not-so-remarkable constant in merger and acquisitions: A business is worth what someone will pay for it, not necessarily what the seller wants.

That tension between the true market value and what the seller thinks a business is worth is something that investment banks like ours have to manage in pretty much every deal we are involved in.

The root of the concern is clear: Some sellers have fantasy company valuations in mind that are not based on historical revenues or trailing EBITDA. Those sellers want to be rewarded for future revenues and future EBITDA, which are by no means guaranteed to materialize. Just as when someone is selling their home, and it is special to them, it doesn't make the place worth more than a neighbor's house of the same size. So too, business owners often have an attachment to their business, and think they are special. Here too, that special attachment is usually expressed as an inflated idea of what the business is worth.

Before we proceed, let's backfill on some basics. Most companies that are acquired have been valued by a multiple of historical EBITDA, typically a *trailing twelve-month* time period. This multiple of EBITDA is determined by dividing the total enterprise value (T.E.V.) paid for the company by the EBITDA. The formula looks like this: *TEV/EBITDA = multiple paid.* For example, if a company sells for $10 million and it had an EBITDA of $2 million, then the multiple paid was 5X, or $10 million / $2 million = 5.

(By the way, if the company being acquired has no EBITDA currently, but has a history of revenues, a.k.a. "top line," a company might be bought on a *multiple of revenues*, typically discounted — often heavily — from what would have been paid if the company were profitable. Acquiring a company that is not profitable is a high-risk investment, since it is nearly impossible to predict how well a company will perform in the future with any degree of certainty. Accordingly, those company values will reflect that uncertainty, compared to a company with around the same top line, but with strong EBITDA.)

In an economy that's at risk of a downturn or recession, or perhaps when an owner is simply exhausted with running a company, it's only natural that a company owner who wants to take his chips off the table will call up an investment banker and say, "I'd like to test the market by putting my company up for sale."

If our investment bank receives that call, our first question is this: "Have you considered what value you'd like to obtain in a sale?"

The owner may respond: "Well, I'm around $2 million in EBITDA now, but my projections show that at the end of next year, we will have a $4 million EBITDA. I'd like to base the value on that future EBITDA, since it's such a sure thing. I see that companies like mine are selling for 6X EBITDA, and so, I'd like 6X on that $4 million and sell my company for $22 million."

Yikes. This seller really needs to be more realistic.

In our example, the 6X being paid for profitable companies is being paid on *historical* EBITDA. So, this fellow's company would sell for 6X $2 million, or $12 million, *not* 6X $4 million, or $24 million.

If there is an intrigued acquirer – maybe another business that's been waiting for the chance to snap up a competitor – they might agree with the seller's projections of $4 million in EBITDA, yet not pay on that today. That intrigued acquirer might pay 6X on $2 million, and then pay a series of earn-out payments, based on delivered future performance. But even that is a stretch sometimes. (This is typically agreed to when the seller stays on, or has a succession plan to keep a team in place to achieve the projections.)

When we explain this scenario to sellers who might have a fantasy, high valuation in mind, some simply say that we are wrong, and they look for an investment banker who agrees with them. But it's been our experience that the most sophisticated acquirers have tight rules for acquisition, low appetites for risk, and little appetite for paying a higher multiple in cash at close for performance that is not yet banked. Discipline in valuations paid, with a bias toward historical performance, is the norm, and for good reason: Buyer are interested in sure things, or performance that is as close to a sure thing as possible.

All of that said, it's essential for the seller to go into the sale process with a realistic idea of what the company is worth, supported by their investment banker's thorough research... otherwise, disappointment is all but assured.

"I cannot give you the formula for success, but I can give you the formula for failure. It is: Try to please everybody." — Herbert Bayard Swope

Chapter 21

Acquiring New Leadership Can Ding Your Valuation

Many executive leaders of private companies are often owners or significant shareholders, and an acquisition is a natural time for them to cash out, or even to take their feet off the gas under new ownership once a deal is closed (and their financial security is assured). Without proper planning, those leaders that are departing, or who wish to remain but whose waning enthusiasm may be detected by an acquirer, can be quite pricey for you as a seller, and this situation should be yet another reason to engage in leadership continuity planning far in advance of a sale.

Here's why: If you are the seller, and you wait too long to replace executive leaders who will leave just after the deal closes, you might very well get docked for the replacement cost (salaries and benefits) of departing key team members, *and* potentially even the costs of replacement talent acquisition through a headhunter.

Give that these costs can have a *negative valuation multiplier effect*, the financial punishment can be quite severe. Zapping $200,000 off your EBITDA to put in place, say, a missing CFO's compensation package too close to a sale can lower a company's valuation by $1.2 million if the company is being valued at 6X EBITDA.

In the absence of leadership continuity or well-planned succession planning, acquirers will consider devaluing (sometimes *severely* devaluing) a leaderless or thinly led company. It should come as no surprise that acquirers want as little churn or disruption as possible when a deal close. Their aim is an *operational steady-state* that doesn't suffer in ownership transition. So, this devaluation can potentially knock *multiple turns* off the valuation calculation, driving down the multiple from 6X EBITDA to 5X or 4X. In fact, if the acquirer realizes during due diligence that they are going to end up with the husk of a company, they might even consider entirely walking away.

The product lineup, the customer base, and that nifty website… Sure, those things are necessary, but they can be decidedly secondary in a valuation equation to solid leadership. Acquirers surely want those branded assets, and a great employee culture besides, but that's just a baseline; moreover, you're naïve to think these company features can be delivered by just anyone.

In every deal our firm has even been involved in, prudent sellers and shrewd acquirers make it a priority to ensure that the leadership (and often the middle management) which made the company attractive enough to acquire are retained after the deal closes to provide leadership to take the company forward.

That means far more than just keeping a few name plates on C-suite doors. It demands that able leaders remain in place to retain the workplace culture, customer relationships, vendor relationships (and a myriad list of other intangibles) to ensure the continued success of an operation.

Some acquirers even want to see the trailing financials *during which the future leaders of the company had significant authority*. Naturally, if an acquirer likes those financials, they'll want to keep the leadership that put up those numbers. If not, all bets may be off.

Keep in mind that putting a solid team in place can be a long process. As a seller, if you've made the wrong hire, you need enough time to determine if a particular hire was ill-advised. (*Harvard Business Review* reports that Fortune 500 leaders run about 50% success rate on hiring decisions!)

Next, be sure to prudently communicate the acquisition news, to ensure stability at every organizational level. When an acquisition is about to take place (or *while* it is taking place), news of the deal should not come as a surprise to the seller company's leadership. That said, it may be prudent to keep the news from rank-and-file employees until a well-planned, sequential announcement strategy is put in place, e.g., Ownership → Leadership → Employees → Customers → Vendors → the Public/Press. If this is not done properly, you can only imagine the damage control you'd have to do if you suddenly broke the news to the management team that the company has been sold. Some might even walk off resentful they weren't kept in the loop; others will wonder if they had not been told because the ink is still drying on their pink slips.

Bottom line: Acquirers look for a solid and well-articulated succession plan to be in place even before they start drafting the paperwork to make an acquisition; moreover, the absence of a plan should raise general concerns that the target company is truly prepared for an ownership transition.

"The crow that tried to be a cormorant, drowned." – Chinese

proverb

Chapter 22

Losing Control During an Earnout Period

When there is a disagreement between an acquirer and a seller about the value of a company, yet determination to get the deal done, an earnout is often put in place. The earnout essentially defers some of the purchase price to a future time (typically one year), and it is paid after the acquired company achieves certain performance goals. For example, let's say that 20% of the purchase price is deferred for 12 months in an earnout. The buyer and the seller then set the performance targets that must be hit before the earnout payout is triggered. The goals can be tied to overall sales, retention of customers, as well as other factors, but they are much more likely to be tied to EBITDA. That is the true indication of the profitability of the company, the very origin of the phrase *the bottom line*.

Earnouts are typically put in place for a period of time when the seller(s) remain in a place in a management role under new ownership, when they are highly motivated indeed to achieve the earnout performance goals, because a big check awaits.

At the time the deal closes, there is often a great deal of optimism about the future prospects of the company. The new owners may be bringing expertise, new management, resources, buying power, and alliances to bear to help the acquired company along. But here's a common point of friction in earned-out deals: The sellers, who is deprived of the powers of outright ownership, may see that the very resources required to achieve the earnout are restricted by the new owners. For instance, the new owners may restrict the marketing budget, cut down on sales staff, reduce the percent of revenue dedicated to trade shows and events, or start charging additional expenses against the seller's budget.

When that happens, it is not uncommon for the sellers to look at the budget and ask each other, "How are we supposed to achieve the target EBITDA when we are down two sales reps, skipping two home shows, and our ad budget is cut 30%?"

What's more, it's only human nature that the sellers might suspect that the constriction of resources might not just be a run-of-the-mill budgeting issue, but a deliberate attempt to deny them what's required to trigger the earnout. The sellers may go to the new owner and appeal, observing, say, that the marketing budget used to be 6% of gross revenues, and now it's only 4% of gross revenues. The new owners might point out that all their other operations run just fine on 4% of gross revenue models, and that is just standard policy, with no ulterior motive whatsoever.

"But what about the fact that you let two sales reps go?" the sellers may ask.

The buyers respond: "Their sales territories overlapped with two of our top guys, and we didn't want the overlap."

The sellers are left stymied and frustrated, as they see the chances dwindle for that last big check.

There are two tactics for avoiding this problem. One is to negotiation *before* the close, as a covenant of the purchase agreement, that the earnout is not "all or none," which is what the buyers will push for. In other words, the buyer will say, "If you hit that $2 million EBITDA, you get the earnout, but anything under $2 million means no earn out will be paid." The sellers should counter

that if 90% of the $2 million is obtained, 90% of the earnout shall be

paid; 80% achieved, 80% paid, etc. (There can be lots of creativity

and "horse trading" around these payment structure, e.g., 90% of the

$2 million achieved, then 75% of the earnout is paid; 80% of $2

million achieved, then 50% of the earnout is paid, etc.)

The second tactic is to set the coming year's marketing

budgets and staffing levels *before* the deal closes, so you know

you'll have the resources required to achieve the earnout goals. The

marketing budget may not be set as a dollar amount, but as a percent

of revenues; the events listed out that you know you will attend; the

sales rep's territories spelled out. By knowing in advance what

resources you have to work with, you can focus on performance, and

not on the fact that you were deprived of resources to achieve your

earnout targets.

"Many of life's failures are people who did not realize how close they were to success when they gave up." — Thomas Edison

Chapter 23

Selecting an Operative Timeframe for Valuation

Traditional performance indicators such as EBITDA, OPEX, and COGs are all used in valuing businesses. That said, the most-common method valuing companies is the tried-and-true "multiple of EBITDA" basis. That multiple is calculated as *Total Enterprise Value* (the purchase price) *divided by EBITDA*.

The *multiple of EBITDA* valuation method is so tried-and-true because EBITDA is widely viewed as a proxy for cash flow, and this method is preferred over, say, basing a company's value on a multiple of top-line revenue or discounted cash flow. Yet, even when applying the multiple of EBITDA method, a company's value depends on the *operative time frame* that an acquirer will agree to when examining financial statements to determine the EBITDA on which the multiple is applied.

Let's take an example: If the operation for sale is in a high-growth phase and located in a great market with strong future prospects, that company could be valued using *future* revenues, or at least expect some consideration for them. This is especially likely if the company has predictable, recurring income, long-time stable customers, and a strong brand. By comparison, a company that is showing flat growth or slow growth would probably have its value based on historical financial performance. For slow-growth / flat-growth companies, acquirers like to look back three years. Some buy-side analysts will *average* the EBITDA across a span of time, and apply a multiple to that average number.

Now, here's a third scenario: If the company for sale is having a relatively good year, taking advantage of strong demand in their products and services, it can be argued (typically by your investment banker) that the acquirer look just at TTM (*trailing twelve months*) to determine the EBITDA used to determine value. If the TTM EBITDA (*wow, we are throwing around the acronyms now!*) is showing a growth trajectory, and your performance convinces the acquirer that this growth will continue, it's fair to ask for a slight premium on the multiple to reflect your good prospects. A slight premium could be moving from, say, 6X EBITDA to a 6.5X EBITDA.

That 0.5X "premium" can add up to be real dollars, either in the pocket of the seller…or out of the pocket of the acquirer. So, expect some, shall we say, *high-functioning conversations* when the seller and acquirer meet to determine exactly what the multiple is.

Let's do the math to determine the implications. For ease of calculation, let's say your company has a $2 million EBITDA over the trailing twelve months. A 6X on that EBITDA would value your company at $12 million. But if you successfully argue that there should be a slight bump of 0.5X in the valuation calculation, citing your growth trajectory, that $12 million purchase price turns into $13 million (6.5 x $2 million = $13 million), a million dollar incremental bonus.

Ok, now let's say that you cite your TTM performance, and argue for a slight premium on the multiple of EBITDA paid for your company. (There's never any harm in asking, but have your investment banker build the case, based on empirical evidence and financial statements. Don't just say it's a gut call!) Your potential acquirer might look over your request and offer an earnout, saying: "Tell you what: I agree with you that your company could be worth 6.5X, but I'd like to hedge my risk. I'll pay you 6X on your TTM EBITDA today, and then I'll pay you 6.5X on the incremental positive EBITDA over the next twelve months. If your company performs as you say it will, then you will end up with higher purchase price. If you don't grow as fast as you project, then you have to settle for the 6X we paid at closing."

This is a perfect example of how the earnout serves as a risk allocation vehicle that stakes, at least in part, the total enterprise value (TEV) paid for your company to your future growth, while also fairly rewarding your proven historical performance.

Note that some earnouts go for more than one year. Sometimes they go as long as three years. But longer duration earnouts mean that you share risk with the acquirer, since there is no way to guarantee what will happen to the economy over an extended period of time.

"The only place where success comes before work is in the dictionary." — Vidal Sassoon

Chapter 24

Why Strategic Investors Pay More

In the broadest scope, there are really only two types of acquirers for your business: 1) **strategic acquirers** that will fold an acquisition into their existing operations, with an aim to achieve synergy, and 2) **non-strategic acquirers** that are buying a company simply to enjoy the cash flow of a portfolio company. This second category of acquirer, the non-strategic type (often a private equity group) can easily become a strategic investor if they acquire, say, a collection of retail outlets, and treat them as a "platform" on which to build. They might add "bolt-on" companies, like a distribution company, or a lumber mill, or a plant to produce decking, siding, or roofing.

Why draw a distinction between these two types of acquirers? The reason is that they pay different multiples of EBITDA when making the acquisition. The strategic acquirer will typically pay a 1X higher multiple of EBITDA than a non-strategic. (We will look at the value implications of that in a minute.)

When our firm engages a client, we are always working for the sellers seeking to be acquired. In the parlance of the industry, that role is called a "sell-side rep," and any sell-side rep worth their salt will run an analysis early-on to estimate the value of the company they are taking to market. (This is done as much to set expectations of the seller as it is to establish an acceptable target range of what to expect from an acquirer.) That valuation estimate typically means searching a database of *recent* deals to see the contemporary multiple of what's been paid for similar companies. (Our firm subscribes to GF Data for this deal information; there are many other similar services.). When we look at the multiple of EBITDA recently paid in an acquisition, we always add 1X to that figure if the buyer is a strategic acquirer.

The strategic acquirer will pay more simply because they see an immediate opportunity to leverage the new acquisition to accelerate growth, leverage synergies, and basically make more money with the conjoined operations than these companies can make if they had worked independently. For example, it only stands to reason that a building products manufacturing company might see the potential synergies – e.g. higher margins, cutting out the middle man – if it were to buy a series of outlets stores, where they can offer their house brand. That's a classic strategic acquisition. Next, the manufacturer that owns the retail outlets might see a compelling reason to own a trucking and logistics company, which would obviate the next natural acquisition of… well, you get the idea. This is how empires are made.

What are the value implications of a strategic acquirer versus a non-strategic acquirer? It's simple math. Let's say a company that seeks to be acquired is booking, for ease of math, $5 million in EBITDA. If a non-strategic acquirer would purchase that company at 5X, they are paying $25 million. If a strategic acquirer is making the acquisition at 6X, they are paying $30 million, a $5 million positive lift for the seller. This higher value is achieved simply because the strategic acquirer can do more with the business it is acquiring than, say, a private equity group that simply wants to harvest the cash flow and let the acquisition sit there as a stand-alone portfolio company.

A final reason that strategics pay more is that they tend to want to hold on to their acquisition, folding it into an integrated operation. Strategics have a bias for the long game. A private equity group / non-strategic, almost invariably, wants to acquire a company, build it up over time, and sell it down the road for a higher value, typically after 3-5 years. They don't have much of an attachment to the company in the cold calculation of the right time to sell it to achieve their target of return on investment.

Bottom line here? Shop your company among strategics first, see if you get nibble (or a bidding war!), and then shop to the non-strategics in a second phase of outreach.

"If you are not embarrassed by the first version of your product, you've launched too late." — *Reid Hoffman, co-founder of LinkedIn*

Chapter 25

Why Companies Sell for Less, or Don't Sell at All

Sometimes, that bright shiny idea you had – to sell your business and feast on the after-tax payout as a reward for your life's work – can become a tarnished penny if you put your company on the market and it doesn't sell, or you get offers far below what you expected. In almost any economic period, recession or booming times, we will hear of deals that receive offers at multiples *below* what have been industry standards. Why aren't these companies getting top dollar, or sometime not selling at all? Here are a few reasons:

1) **Recession**. Acquirers are often pricing in a "future recession," or at least using that as a reason for offering a low price. A recession is *always* surely in our future, at

some time. It's an unavoidable part of natural business cycles, as much as a recession may be forestalled by goosing the economy with tax cuts and adjustments to interest rates. Since an acquirer is likely going to maintain ownership of your business for a number of years, they are actively modeling how it will perform in a downturn. Essentially, they are not buying the company for how it is performing today; they are pricing in how it will perform over near-term time periods under their new ownership. Since there are so many variables that they can't predict, they are hedging their risk by offering less, playing defense against potential slower performance.

2) **Margins.** Prudent acquirers are very careful to target companies whose gross profit margin and EBITDA margins are around the same as theirs (or ideally *higher*). Especially in tight-margin or low-margin business sectors, even 2 or 3 percentage points off expected EBITDA performance can sour an acquirer's appetite for the purchase, or motivate them to reduce the multiple of EBITDA they're willing to pay. This is true not only of

EBITDA margins but of gross profit margins as well. Acquirers will pay a premium only for performance that matches or exceeds their expectations.

3) **Leadership**. Most acquirers will want to examine the EBITDA performance of a target company for a period of time when it was under control of the leadership team that will remain in place, post-acquisition. In other words, if you, as an owner/leader, are leaving the company after you sell it, it's important to implement a succession plan with enough time for the new leadership team to demonstrate their operational ability. If you don't have a succession plan in place, or you installed a new team too close to the sale of the business – allowing no time for a prove-out – expect a haircut on valuation. Worse, if you have no succession plan at all, and the incoming new owner gets even a whiff that your leaders are jumping ship after the acquisition, expect a *buzz cut*; actually expect your head to get shaved! You may even find that the acquirer completely walks away from the deal.

4) **Aging equipment**. We often see companies that have taken money out of the business, when they should have re-invested in modernizing equipment, building upkeep, and regular maintenance. When equipment isn't maintained, the acquirer will price in the investment they will have to make, and lop that off your EBITDA line as an expense they will incur. Since companies are bought at a multiple of EBITDA, every dollar removed from the EBITDA line has a *negative multiplier effect* on the value of your business. Lack of equipment investment and lack of maintenance are nearly impossible to hide, either during initial site visits, or during the due diligence process. We have seen acquirers walk away from company based solely on the poor equipment quality.

5) **An old fashioned low-ball.** Any businessperson worth his or her salt wants to buy a business on the cheap, and if they sense that an owner just wants to get out (as opposed a seller who exudes patience), the acquirer may throw out a low bid, or a series of low bids during back-and-forth, probing to find "the bottom" of where the owner will go

to simply cash out of the business. So, pro tip: sellers, beware when making comments like, "Oh we just want to get out of it," or "We are not looking for the top of the market here," because that's music to an aggressive savvy acquirer's ears.

If you are not sure why you are getting such a low bid, why not just ask?

"What gives?" might be too blunt a way to express your frustration, but you can say something like: "Your bid is below our expectations. We are just curious why you are outside the normal range of valuation multiples for a company as successful as ours. What's the reason?" That question might just open up a more candid exchange that results in a deal value that "meets in the middle" through compromise on both sides, the buyer and the seller.

"There is no greater agony than bearing an untold story inside you." —*Maya Angelou*

Chapter 26

That's Not a Downward Trend! Let's Normalize Revenues

One of the worst red flags for an acquirer is when they see your revenues drop in the year you sell your company, when compared to the previous year. Even worse is the following scenario: You show a good solid symmetrical increase in revenues over a *number of years,* only to have revenues go soft just before a sale.

For example, assume that you want to sell your company this year. Looking back over three years financials, let's say that your company booked $20 million three years ago, then $22 million two years ago, and then – a banner year! – $27 million last year.

That's a nice growth path. You added $2 million and then $5 million to your revenue. What's not to like?

But let's also say that in the year of sale your revenues *declined* to $26 million. Even though your company has experienced solid gains in revenue growth – moving from $20 to $26 million over three years – it appears as though your revenues are *falling* from $27 million to $26 million year-over-year at the time of sale.

Since we obviously don't have data about next year's sales, a $1 million drop is sales year-over-year will be perceived as the *beginning of a downward trend* by an acquirer that is looking for any reason to lower the purchase price of your company.

How do you argue for maximum valuation, when your company seems to be losing market share? The answer: Normalizing your revenues.

In a situation like this, your investment banker should dig deeply into the reasons why your $27 million year was so strong…and an anomaly. Maybe a huge order came in that was unusual. That one-time occurrence was a fantastic boost in your revenues. Let's say it was $3 million in unexpected revenue. You know it was a "sugar high" that may not repeat, but why should you be punished in the valuation of your business just because of this one-time event?

The best approach to take is to have your investment banker write an explanation of this in the *informational memorandum* (the document that describes all your operations and financials). The investment banker should make a bar chart or infographic that shows that what's *really* happening to your company is the following: You are growing at the rate of $2 million a year. You booked $20 million three years ago, $22 million two years ago, $24 million (*normalized*) last year, and $26 million this year.

Inevitably the acquirer will say, "Wait, you didn't book $24 million last year. Says right here in the financials that you booked $27 million!"

You and your investment banker should respond: "We actually booked $24 million in a *normalized revenue projection* and – as you can see with this evidence we have presented – a huge one-time project gave us an anomalous boost of $3 million in revenue."

Since you are not going to have your valuation pegged to last year's revenue (or only partially so), it actually behooves you to

show symmetrical $2 million increases rather than to reveal a
phantom "downward trend" in revenues represented by the "drop"
from $27 million to $26 million.

Why wouldn't you want to take credit for that sugar high of
on unusual incremental $3 million boost in revenue? Isn't it better to
just own that as evidence that, well, it might happen again?

As nice as it is to show such strong recent revenues, acquirers
want revenues and growth that are *sustainable*. The sustainability
allows them to plan and predict. If they know that a company will
increase sales by $2 million a year, that's marginally more attractive
from a planning point of than revenues that are asymmetrical, up one
year, down the next.

All of that said, can you get credit for a $3 million flush of
orders from another new development in your service area? You
certainly can. In the informational memorandum, an experienced
investment banker will have surveyed forthcoming new projects /
planned projects, and baked in the possibility of you obtaining that
work in the future. Although those future jobs are not nearly as
valuable as actual booked revenue, they show promise for your
markets, and that should help infuse a sense of optimism in the mind

of the acquirer, which will probably affect the valuation in positive

way.

"You get in life what you have the courage to ask for." — *Oprah Winfrey*

Chapter 27

A Culture of Safety is Key to an Acquisition

(This following chapter might apply just to more traditional manufacturing and distribution businesses, and not high tech.)

I once did a site walk-through with a potential acquirer – actually an entire team sent in from the acquirer – and they wanted to look over the grounds of my client (a manufacturing wholesaler and dealer), before making an offer for the company. When you get to this stage in the acquisition process, where there's a site visit taking place, it's fairly exciting. The site visit usually indicates strong buyer interest, and the increased likelihood that a *letter of intent* may follow soon after. After all, no one incurs the expense of flying a whole team across the country for a site visit without serious intentions.

This particular location had working garage bays that contained loud machinery that was part of the operation, and you could hear the machines screaming in the background from everywhere on site. The prospective acquirer's team were all adorned with ear protection, hard hats, and safety glasses. But as we walked into the work area, it was clear that none of the workers were wearing any protection. Not for their eyes, ears, or heads.

I cringed. We'd warned our client, the seller, to get the work site spiffed up for a visit. And they had, but they mainly focused on cleaning up refuge and dunnage piles. It was obvious, and a little too late, for me to realize that this place did not have a *culture of safety*... and the potential acquirer noticed it right away.

To make matters worse, a fork lift drove between us and the building we were walking toward, with a worker hanging casually off the back and, if that wasn't enough, the forklift had one flat tire. It flopped along sadly as I tried to keep my head from exploding.

One of the fellows from the acquirer's team looked at me as he heard the screaming saws, which were booming at 120+ decibels. (Normal hearing is 60 decibels, and the threshold to avoid hearing loss is 8 hours at >85DB *average*.)

"No ear protection?" he shouted, gesturing to the workers.

I signaled over the noise that this was something we could correct under new ownership.

He shouted over the noise again: "If we buy this company, we will immediately do a baseline hearing test to establish the damage baseline for *all* the workers."

What was he afraid of? One word: *Lawsuits*.

Under new ownership, it would be entirely possible for the workers to sue the new owners, who largely assume these liabilities. The workers could claim that not enough was done to prevent their hearing loss. Or eye injuries. Or head injuries. The fact that forklifts were roaring around with flat tires and workers catching rides didn't exactly give the potential acquirers confidence that they were buying a safety-driven / safety-first operation. In addition to the worker's well-being, this work site was one OSHA inspection away from a citation and fines… another potential liability for the new owner as well.

In the end, the prospective buyer elected not to bid on the company for acquisition. There were additional reasons they elected not to make the acquisition, but I can assure you that safety issue was one of them. Maybe not the first one, but certainly a contributing factor.

If you are taking your company to market, one area that should clearly be addressed is your safety programs. Is everyone equipped with the right safety gear? Are your sites OSHA complaint? Would you pass an OSHA pop inspection with flying colors? Are you doing all you can to reduce the likelihood of future lawsuits over preventable health problems now?

Moreover, can you prove that you have a culture of safety and regulatory compliance, with a documented record of safety meetings, and even a safety officer (maybe not full-time, but a designee who knows the rules). These are items that potential acquirer will look for, not only out of human concern for workers, but to limit their liability should an injury occur after they've taken ownership, or should claims of damaged health arise in the months and years after the new owner has assumed control.

Your safety procedures should be spelled out in your offering document, which is called an *Informational Memorandum* (or "IM"), so it's clear what documented steps you've taken to limit your own liability and to limit the potential liability of the new owner.

"I am not a product of my circumstances. I am a product of my decisions." – Stephen Covey

Chapter 28

Always Shop the Deal. (*Almost* Always.)

Our firm took a company to market for acquisition recently, and it sold the first day. "Sold," in the sense that the buyer identified themselves in a phone call, saying, *"We're the buyer,"* before we could get a word in edgewise. *"We're the buyer,"* they said again, before we even had a chance to ask who exactly was calling.

The excitement was palpable. We were all thrilled. A market-clearing price was set, and the due diligence process started in earnest the next day.

In this case, the acquirer knew the company we took to market for acquisition. They knew the leadership, and they owned a complementary company that made the synergies very valuable to them. In fact, they had been lying in wait, just itching for our client company to come on the market, and when they did, *boom!*, magic happened. They weren't going to let this one slip away. They didn't want anyone else to even see the deal, and we turned away other inquiries who were working off the deal teaser.

Is that common? Unfortunately, it's not. It's rare.

That said, you never know who your buyer will be, and it's imperative that – short of accepting a market-clearing price – you take the offering of your company as far and wide as possible.

First of all, what's a market-clearing price? That's the price that you, as the owner, know you'd be happy to get for your company in an all-cash-at-close deal. Not a so-called "fantasy valuation," but a realistic number in the high range of what's reasonable. The market-clearing price should never make you feel regret, nor have you mumbling later, "Gosh, I wonder if I'd only shopped around, maybe I could have gotten more…"

So, short of a market-clearing offer by an acquirer, you really want your investment banker to take the deal as far and wide as possible. And that means offering the company to people who are clearly unlikely buyers. So, push the deal teaser out to strategic buyers, far and wide; push the deal teaser out to private equity groups and family offices. You never know when a deal will catch someone's imagination. And keep in mind that as big as we think the world is, most business communities are actually quite small. People talk. "Did you see that company for sale? I bet I know who that is. You know who might be interested in that, my friend over at XYZ. I'm going to call him to make sure he's seen this."

That's the advantage of making a broad reach.

Additionally, shopping a deal accomplishes two other things, in addition to reaching a network of buyers, or companies that might refer the buyer: It creates *deal buzz*, and you want that out there. Even though the deal teaser doesn't identify your company by name, people *always* start the guessing game when the teaser starts making the rounds. And deal buzz can really be a motivator, putting a little bit of fear in companies they might start to worry if they risk missing out on something, such as a chance to buy a pesky competitor who's been driving them crazy.

The second thing the deal buzz does is to create a sense of *deal urgency*, so there is momentum to collect *letters of intent* (LOIs), and drive toward accepting an offer, followed by a rapid due diligence process.

A sense of urgency is a key part of mergers and acquisitions because the last thing you want is a deal without momentum. When an acquirer raises their hand and is selected as the winning bid, you want to parley their excitement to fuel momentum through due diligence, and drive toward a close. The worst thing is when you land a buyer, they're excited to get the deal done, and then for whatever reason – legal hick ups, request for re-pricing, questions of management salary adjustments, environmental audits – the deal stalls between the LOI phase and the closing. That's when everyone can go driven crazy, wondering who's in charge. (Candidly, in times like those, it takes real leadership on the investment banker's part to serve as task master and keep the deal moving along.)

Bottom line: Widely shop your deal, create the buzz, and leverage the excitement into momentum to get the deal closed.

If you don't ask, the answer is always no. — Nora Roberts

Chapter 29

Beware Financial Engineering

We took a successful, growing company to market recently, and a buyer quickly stepped up with a verbal offer to pay a premium over what the owners expected for their company, while asking that it be taken off the market. The buyer wanted to halt the offering from being shown to others, as they put forth a market-clearing price. Their underlying motive was to avoid competing with other acquirers in bidding wars that might emerge in a controlled auction.

This offer (a.k.a. a "pre-empt") had a wow factor, make no mistake. The sellers said the price was right. We invited the acquirer to reveal the deal structure. That's when it started to unravel.

For this example, let's say that this potential acquirer wanted to pay $20 million for the target company on a cash-free/debt-free basis. Let's also assume the target company was operating at a $2 million EBITDA. The company's projections were attractive and realistic, showing $2.5 million in EBITDA in the current year, moving to $3 million and $3.5 million EBITDA in the subsequent two years.

But the offer depended on some clever "financial engineering." First, it's common for acquirers to ask sellers to stay with the company, and put some of equity back into the new company. Let's say that the acquirer asked the sellers to leave behind 10% each, totaling 20%. Right away, the potential acquirer reduced the cash required at close by 20% of their $20 million offer, leaving them with $16 million to come up with.

Next, while working to minimize their cash requirements, the acquirer then offered to put down $7 million in cash-at-close. (Based on the target company's strong balance sheet, most of the $7 million would have been raised through senior debt and mezzanine financing, which would end up on the balance sheet of the company post-close. In effect, the buyer had to put up very little of their own money to buy the company for a $20 million valuation.)

But with $7 million in cash, that still means they had to make up the "missing" $9 million of the offer.

Ok, just to recap, the potential acquirer offered $20 million, minus the owners' equity, so $16 million was required. Then, deduct the $7 million cash-at-close, and just $9 million was required. Where did they propose that comes from?

The potential acquirer then proposed paying $9 million over three years, an earnout, in this manner (tied to performance metrics): $2.5 million in the first year, $3 million in the second year, and $3.5 million in the third year, for a total of $9 million. You'll note that these figures are identical to the projected EBITDA for the next three years.

Does This Look Fishy?

Does this look fishy? Yes, it does. Here's why: The potential acquirer was using financial engineering in an attempt to obtain a $20 million company by risking very little of their own money. After the sellers leave behind their equity in the new company, the potential acquirer is essentially paying for the business out of the future proceeds of the business.

What's off here is that the sellers are really getting only $7 million in "guaranteed money," *plus* the future value of their equity, but that's in a company they will no longer control. In the clear light of day, you realize that the sellers are being asked to allow money they would have taken as disbursements (three future years of EBITDA) to pay themselves for their own company...all while giving up ownership!

Further adding to the risk profile of this offer, the buyers are likely going to put covenants in the purchase agreement that state the earnouts will be made only if the company achieves certain performance metrics. Whereas the seller should always tie that performance to top-line revenue, or gross profit dollars, buyers typically want it tied to EBITDA. However, EBITDA is the line item that can be easily manipulated, for instance by adding corporate finance charges by the buyer, making a large marketing expenditure, hiring more sales people, or larding on *selling, general, and administrative* (SG&A) expenses. The EBITDA could easily be driven below the threshold where the earnout payment is triggered.

Make no mistake, the potential acquirer is being quite clever. These types of structures are common, but they are common for companies that are distressed, or are cornered by debt, or are desperate to sell. For successful, growing companies, there is simply no need to allow an acquirer to pay you with your own money. In a case like this, we would advise that you "walk the deal," and find

another structure that has less risk and more cash at close.

"Please think about your legacy, because you're writing it every day." — *Gary Vaynerchuk*

Chapter 30

When is a Deal Priced?

For Growing Companies, Price a Deal Just Before You Close

When you are being acquired, and you and your investment banker start to receive *letters of intent* (LOIs), those LOIs will set out a framework for pricing your company. In most LOIs, a dollar amount is offered for your company, but it is always either the result of a multiple of EBITDA, or it can be backed into a multiple-of-EBITDA formula. If the LOI states that the target company will be acquired for $6 million, and the company has a $1 million EBITDA, the company is being valued at 6X. That said, most companies seek acquisition when they are on an upward trend, putting up numbers each month that are higher than the previous month. This month-over-month improvement is an ideal trend to show an acquirer.

151

(Obviously, companies that are growing are highly desirable and get the highest value, as opposed to companies that are coasting along, doing the same business volume month after month, or companies that are contracting.) But if your company is showing month-over-month improvement, and the acquirer reveals the multiple of EBITDA they are using in the valuation within their LOI, at what point in time do you "freeze" the EBITDA to apply the multiple? Do you do it at the time the LOI is submitted? Or based on last year's financial statements? Or based on rolling trailing twelve month reports?

Let's say you are selling your company in the middle of a fiscal year. For a business that is growing, you would be leaving money on the table in terms of your business value if you accepted an LOI that applied the multiple-of-EBITDA valuation method to last year's financials. That would not fully credit intervening months of solid performance. To show you the impact of the math, let's say that your previous fiscal year's EBITDA was $1 million, which would value your company at $6 million in a 6X formula. Now, let's say that six months into the new fiscal year, your trailing twelve-month EBITDA shows improvement, and it's $1.2 million.

Instead of $6 million, the 6X formula would value your company at $7,200,000... a $1.2 million lift in business value. (Just about enough extra to pay the gains tax and net out $6 million!)

To put an even finer point on it, some acquirers of growing companies will want to freeze the EBITDA to which the multiple is applied on the date the LOI is accepted. Let's say you are at $1.2 million in trailing twelve-month EBITDA in July when the LOI is submitted and accepted. The offer comes in at $7.2 million. But the due diligence and closing process can easily take 90 days. If you are a growing company, during those 90 days, your trailing twelve-month EBITDA might climb still higher. Say it rises to a trailing twelve month $1.3 million. Why would you take $7.2 million when the value was frozen at the acceptance of the LOI, when you really should be pricing the deal of 6X $1.3, or $7.8 million? That's $600,000 over the value that would have been paid just 90 days earlier.

The ideal timing of the deal pricing for growing companies should be as close to the closing as possible, so you don't lose the incrementally positive deal value generated during the due diligence process.

That said, when you agree with the buyer to price near the date of the closing, there is risk. Let's say that at the time you accept an LOI based on 6X EBITDA, you are performing at that $1.2 million EBITDA on trailing twelve-month basis. But you and your investment banker negotiate for a pricing that happen 90 days later. Let's also say that, oh take something really crazy, a freak pandemic sweeps through the country shutting down businesses, and you come off the mark, dropping from $1.2 million TTM EBITDA to $1.1 million. The deal value drops from $7.2 to $6.6 million. And perhaps two months later, the pandemic is still around, and you drop to $950,000 EBITDA. The deal value has now moved from the $7.2 million offered in the LOI to $5.7 million. So, when you agree to price close to closing, do everything you can to ensure that you are climbing into that event, not fighting a rear-guard action to assure the acquirer that you are "just having a couple bad months," because at that point the buyer holds all, or most of, the cards and can request "repricing after LOI," a topic we have covered earlier in this book.

"Don't let the fear of losing be greater than the excitement of winning." —

Robert Kiyosaki

Chapter 31

How Cash and Debt Are Blended in an Acquisition

Our first relies on a databased from GF Data), which reviews recent successful acquisitions. One metric they track is "equity" (cash out into the deal), and two types of debt (senior debt and mezzanine debt a.k.a. "subordinate debt") are blended in typical mid-market deals. As its name implies, *senior debt* is the "first-in-line" debt that a company must repay if it goes out of business (liquidation or bankruptcy). Subordinate-debt has less security, and if a company goes out of business, "sub-debt" ranks behind senior debt in repayment priority. As a result, sub-debt costs more to borrow (higher interest rate), because it prices in that risk.

In most acquisition,, there is a blend of these three classes of capital – equity, senior debt, and sub-debt. But what are the typical percentages of each that make up the overall TEV (total enterprise value)? In a recent GF Data deport, of the *total enterprise values* examined, 40.5% of the TEV was *senior debt*. This debt was loaded on to the books of the acquired company; the company will pay the premium and principle out of its income. For these same companies, 13% of the TEV was *subordinate debt;* it too was loaded on the books of the acquired company. Just 46.5% – *less than half* the TEV – was actual equity, in the form of cash.

To put this another way, it is common for us to hear this question: "How much leverage was placed on the deal?" Well, in the acquisitions in this recent GF Data report, that leverage is 40.5% + 13%, for a total of 53.5%. More than half the deal value was, in essence, provided by the balance sheet of the acquired company.

As for the equity portion of the TEV paid, the type of acquirer will dictate where that cash comes from. Specifically, it is common for private equity acquirers to require that a certain percent of the equity be rolled by the seller, in the form of shares, into the NewCo being created. What portion of the TEV is typically required from the seller? It can be as much as 50% of the *equity portion* of the deal. If the seller contributes 50% of the required equity by rolling their shares into NewCo, that would represent around 23% of the TEV being paid.

So, of the 46.5% equity portion of the TEV cited in the chart, the actual cash that the private equity acquirer has to come up with is just 23.5% of the total enterprise value! Less than a quarter of the deal. (Nice work if you can get it, right?) The rest is seller-financed or debt-financed. This blend of 1) senior debt, 2) sub-debt, 3) the rolling of the seller's shares seller, and 4) cash from the acquirers is extremely common.

As opposed to private equity acquirers, strategic buyers usually *don't want* strategic investors that are hold-overs from previous ownership. So, strategic buyers will often *not require* the rolling of the seller's shares, because they don't want the sellers around, or at least they don't want them to have shareholder power to influence the strategic direction of the NewCo. So, strategics will often pony up the equity portion of the deal to cleanly buy the sellers out.

"Even skillful hands can't hold water." — *Asian Proverb*

Chapter 33

Time is the Enemy in Deal Making

They say you should never buy clothes (especially festive shirts) on vacation that you plan to wear back home. Yes, I know, you're strolling the beach shops and you spot that nifty little number. And even though your traveling companion says, "Are you sure you're going to wear that once we get home?" You shake your head: "Of course I will! That party at the Davis' last Easter, I would have worn this very shirt!"

And your partner says: "And you don't think Mrs. Davis would be offended by all the skulls on the collar?"

"No way," you insist as you head to the cash register.

Of course, a week later, unpacking your bags, you pull out that skull shirt, and say, "What in the name of Jehovah was I thinking!?" Turning to your companion you say: "Why didn't you stop me?"

To which they say: "Don't you hate it that I'm always right?"

Yes, you're experiencing *buyer's regret.* In the cold light of day, a week after you closed your shirt deal, you look at the item and think: *What came over me to pay so much for this? Why did I think this was a good fit?*

On vacation, it's not just shirts that you buy that look odd later. I'm sure more than a few readers of this column have looked around that nice ski condo you rented and said, "Why don't we just buy this place, and come here all the time?" To which your companion says: "Don't you remember it took us 13 hours to get here, and you were cursing the traffic on I-70 as soon as we left the rental car lot?"

Well, this same over-enthusiasm to make a purchase, and the ensuing buyer's regret, can also happen in deal making when you offer your business for sale, and it's something you, as a seller, should take advantage of.

Here's how: An acquirer spots your business, gets the deal book from your investment banker, and then – all of a sudden – there's a rush of conference calls.

They're thrilled you've come on the market!

They've been watching you for some time; you're a perfect fit for their portfolio!

Site visits are hurriedly planned. When you meet, your teams get along fabulously. Turns out you know the same people, the same vendors. Some of your employees worked with theirs at past jobs. You all get a feeling of brotherhood when shaking hands as the visit wraps.

Sure enough, the buyer has fast-tracked an LOI, and boom, you have an offer. It's a strong one! The team that visited your site reported back about all the synergies that are possible in a tie-up, thinking of what the combined buying power will do for margins.

As a seller, at this point, you want to take advantage of that enthusiasm. First, don't get cocky on the price. If the offer is strong – even if it's not entirely what you wanted – consider accepting it. Above all, if you are offered a strong $12 million, don't sit back and say: "Hmm, if they offered $12, maybe I can get $13. Or maybe someone else would offer $14!" When you ask for $14, there's a chance the buyer will walk, mumbling about how unrealistic you are to expect that much.

Second, if you go back and bog down the LOI redline markups and requests for more money, or onerous employment terms, then time is your enemy, and the buyer has a chance to rethink the offer. Their enthusiasm may wane in the cold light of day, and – as days drag into weeks or even months – a few of the acquirer's analysts may sit back and say, "Are we overpaying for that company?" Another might add: "You know, they didn't accept our offer right away. It was a *great* offer! Are they really team players? Are they leveraging us against another buyer? Maybe withdraw the LOI?"

And sure enough, we've seen this happen, the dreaded phone call come, when the buyer says, "You know, since you have not signed that LOI yet, we are rethinking our offer. We're going to withdraw that first LOI and offer a second one."

Think it will be a higher price? Nope. It will be lower, or propose increased seller leverage. So, when enthusiasm is running high, consider "riding the wave," and accepting the decent (if not an absolutely 100% perfect) offer, and move expeditiously to the closing before someone says, "Are you really sure what we're buying is a good fit?"

"It is better to act too quickly than it is to wait too long." — Jack Welch

Chapter 33

How to Pocket Cash from Your Balance Sheet in the Sale of Your Company

The vast majority of companies are sold on a debt-free / cash-free basis. In a debt-free / cash-free sale, you the seller must resolve any long-term debt out of the proceeds of the deal at the closing (e.g. family notes, bank notes). The good news is that you get to keep "cash" and "cash equivalents" on your balance sheet. Upon hearing this, many of you are reaching for your phone, and dialing your accountant to ask: *"How much cash do I have on my balance sheet?"*

Your balance sheet may have tons of cash beyond your liabilities; many companies do. But your accountant might come back with a disappointing answer, like this: "Well, we *had* lots of cash three months ago. Then, you made that large inventory purchase because you couldn't pass on the low prices."

You hang up the phone wondering why you didn't take you Mom's advice to become a dentist.

Then you dial your accountant again: "Forgot to ask. How much cash would we have on the balance sheet in six months? That's when the deal would close if we were acquired."

The accountant: "Oh, that's a much better cash position, because you will have sold off that inventory you bulked up on, and if you stick closely to your 12-month inventory average, well, you'll have a healthy cash balance."

You hang up the phone, triumphant: *Ah ha! Who needs dental school, when you can run a business?!"*

The accountant makes a great point. If you see a great deal on materials – and at the time you're *not* really thinking of selling your company – you may be wise to draw down cash to make a purchase. That's a classis buying behavior: Bulk up, sell down over a long period of time. But that may be unwise in the year going into the sale of your company. Let's see why.

Any business owner's inventory management can be measured in four ways, all related to a Days on Hand ("DOH") and inventory turns. Those four metrics are 1) DOH-Month, 2) DOH-Yearly Average, 3) Inventory Turns-Month, and 4) Inventory Turns-On Yearly Average.

If your company has a high Days on Hand, which will invariably lead to "low" Inventory Turns (e.g., below three time/year), you will invariably have cash unnecessarily locked up in inventory that is simply not moving that fast (items #1 and #2 in the list above).

This will probably not be an issue, *if* you are not selling your company. You place big orders a couple times a year at the co-op shows, and then sell down the items over a period of months (see item #3 and #4 above).

Unfortunately, if you have low turns consistently over a period of years, you establish a pattern that a potential acquirer will point to and say: "Your profitability and success seem clearly based on turning inventory 3X/year. Let's maintain that going into the closing." (Secretly, the acquirer is drooling over the prospect of moving to 5X/year and harvesting the extra cash.)

But if you, the seller, want to extract as much cash out of the business at the time of sale, that 3X/year turns pattern will work against you, because you've got so much cash locked up in relatively slow-moving inventory. If you had been buying inventory at a higher frequency / lower volume, you'd have more cash on your balance sheet, subject to harvest at closing.

There are a couple of problems with making a last-minute adjustment to notch up your turns: You can't suddenly "see the light" and convert to higher inventory turns just a month or two before a sale, just to bump up cash reserves. The buyer will perceive that as "out-of-pattern" and suspect (correctly) that you're selling off inventory beyond your normal multi-month averages just to bulk up balance sheet cash at closing. The other problem is your working capital PEG which is typically based on twelve-month averages of your current assets and current liabilities. Lowering inventories several months before the close and the working capital PEG "true-up" could leave you with a negative adjustment to your working capital PEG.

Engage in higher frequency ordering / lower volume / high turns / less cash locked up for *months,* or *a full year* before selling your company, while asking your investment banker to explain the changed behavior to the seller.

Clearly, maximizing cash harvest, at-close, is possible, but seek your investment banker's help in advance to adjust your practice so it is acceptable to the acquirer.

"Every sale has five basic obstacles: no need, no money, no hurry, no desire, no trust." — *Zig Ziglar*

Chapter 34

Already Got a Buyer? Why Even Use an Investment Banker?

Our investment bank will often get a call from a company that has just been approached by an acquirer. The selling company asks for our advice on pricing the deal, and for help with due diligence, documentation, and closing.

Traditionally, it is the investment banker's role to seek out the buyer – through the process of writing the *confidential informational memorandum* ("CIM") and outreach to a list of appropriate buyers. But often a company that hasn't even offered itself for sale gets a phone call to see if they are interested in selling. And that's what happened here.

What possible role can the investment banker play at that point in the process? *Lots!*

Here's how: After we investment bankers have gotten financial statements organized and written the CIM, probably our most-important role is to advise on the *value* of the company for sale and the *structure* of the deal, especially to guard against "over-leveraging" of you, the seller.

With this particular seller, the acquirer was offering a multiple of EBITDA on the previous fiscal year's performance. For ease of math, say it was 6X $2 million, for a *total enterprise value* of $12 million. The seller was inclined to take it. After all, who turns up their noses at $12 million?

We said: *"Wait just one minute!"*

You see, the fiscal year had ended three plus months prior, and the seller had put up solid numbers in the interim time. Our staff CPA immediately did a comparison of the 6X EBITDA for 1) last fiscal year, 2) last calendar year, and 3) *trailing twelve months* ("TTM"), looking for the scenario to bring the highest deal value, since we knew the acquirer's multiple was 6X. We quickly found an additional $200,000 in acceptable EBITDA with just a slight adjustment to the operative EBITDA examination period. With the deal going off at 6X, finding that $200k lifted the company's value by $1.2 million (a premium that more than paid our bank's success fee twice over).

Then we asked to see the balance sheet. Turns out, our client was sitting on a pile of *cash or cash equivalents*; over $1 million dollars. But the acquirer's offer did not make clear it was a cash-free / debt-free deal. In a cash-free / debt-free deal, the seller gets to keep *cash or cash equivalents.* However, that needs to be spelled out. Lacking that clarity, the buyer could have argued for claiming the *cash or cash equivalents* or a portion of them. We advised that the cash-free / debt-free deal structure be explicit in the *asset purchase agreement*, or "APA."

Then there was the seller leverage. The acquirer was asking that the seller loan them part of the money to make the purchase. Crazy as that sounds, it's very common: A "seller note." However, the interest, terms and duration of the note had to be negotiated, since they were overly onerous of the seller. We got that done too.

After getting the price higher, the cash reclaimed, and the seller note negotiated, we then went to work on two more essential parts of any deal: 1) Red-lining the APA, adding seller protections, and 2) Calculating the working capital "peg," to make sure the seller wasn't leaving too much in the cash draw.

Finally, we served as a buffer between our client and the seller. The reason for that is crucial to preserving deal value. Here's why: Acquirers often want to talk directly with sellers and, for lack of a better term, *sweet talk them* with their vision for the company, how well they will treat the employees, and what they will do to protect the brand. Without being disingenuous, these gestures are often sincere, but it's the investment banker's unsentimental take on the deal that will ward off any softening on sales price that might come as a result of these conversations. Because, well, let's face it: At day's end, it's not about vision, it's about the money.

With all of that settled, we moved ahead with traditional due diligence management, troubleshooting document requests, and managing third parties that are often involved, such as outside accounting firms.

Besides all that – and the resulting *seven-figure* lift in purchase price – who ever needs the services of an investment banker when they already have a buyer on the line? Maybe everyone.

"Career advice: Don't sell s!#t you don't want to buy. Don't work for people you don't want to become." — Shane Parrish

Chapter 35

Creative Earn-Out Structures

Even in a hot M&A market, where this is enduring support for strong acquisition values, buyers of companies are not exactly splashing cash around like drunken sailors or newly elected presidents. When discussing deals with a buyer that is about to submit LOIs (*letters of intent*), we consistently hear phrases that sound, more or less, like this: "Well, we certainly are interested, and we know there are other parties circling this deal, but we don't want to over-pay for it."

To manage the risk of potentially overpaying, and to bridge the value perception between buyers and sellers, buyers often use a traditional instrument: An earn-out.

We've seen two creative earn-out strategies recently, one bad for the seller and one good for the seller, and they looked like this, starting with the bad one.

In the first case, the buyer was very cautious. They offered a chunk of cash for the deal at close, around 70% of the purchase price. Then, they spread the remaining 30% over the ensuing three years, when they would pay the seller any EBITDA over a certain dollar amount, *each year*, until the agreed upon purchase price was achieved. If the purchase price was not fully paid out to the seller after three years because of EBITDA shortfall, the seller had to eat the difference. If the buyer paid out the agreed-upon purchase price before the three-year period, they buyer would not pay more than that, even if the EBITDA soared above projections.

This offer, of course, was rejected out of hand. It's ridiculous.

First, it's based on EBITDA dollars. Under a new owner, EBITDA can be easily driven down if the new owner elects to jack up OPEX, with such things as new marketing, new hires, etc. What's to stop the new owner from seeing their exposure on an upcoming earn-out payment, and simply drive up expenses to reduce (even to zero) the amount due to the seller? Second, a three year earn-out is overlong. You really should aim for one year, because who's to say how the business will be run under new management two and three years hence. There's way too much risk for the seller here.

A second earn-out we saw was much more collaborative and accommodating to the seller, and we accepted it. The total potential earnout was $2 million. It could be achieved in just one year, not three. And it was based on gross profit dollars, not EBITDA, which is something we insist on for all our clients.

It was structured like this: Since we were projecting that our client, the seller, would grow at 25% in the first year of new ownership, the buyer said, "Once you reach last fiscal year's gross profit dollar figure, we will pay out $1.25 for every gross profit dollar above that, until the $2 million is fully paid."

Note that the ".25" in the $1.25 is the projected growth rate.

In any earn-out, a buyer won't pay for zero year-over-year growth. Not surprisingly, this buyer's proposed earn-out pays *only* for year-over-year growth. They are paying a fair premium on every dollar above last fiscal year's gross profit, while putting an incentive in place for the sellers to blow through the projections as fast as possible. In fact, if the seller really "blew the bloody doors off" their performance, they could achieve the earn-out before the end of the year, reducing the jitters everyone experiences when there are millions at stake.

Quick review: When negotiating earn-outs, always base them on gross profit dollars; contain the period to max one-year; and structure the earn-out so the buyer can hedge their risk, yet reward you, the seller, for the growth that exceeds last year's performance.

" Even honey / tastes like medicine / when it's medicine " — Asian Proverb

Chapter 36

Don't Take Low Offers Personally

A neighborhood friend stormed into my house recently, fuming. He'd just put his house on the market and gotten a bid the very first day. The realtor told him the bidder was his next-door neighbor.

That's not what upset him. It was the bid. It was really low. Below the house's listing price.

He ranted: "I can't believe that anyone, to say nothing of my next-door neighbor, would try to low-ball me!"

I stared at this friend in quiet amazement. I said: "Sit down my son. Let me tell you how the world actually works. First, don't take a low bid personally. Even though the bidder knows you, that doesn't mean he's going to give you free money just because you're a nice guy. He's just trying to find the bottom of the price range."

"Secondly," I continued, "the bidder is working on asymmetrical knowledge. His bid is the first step in 'gaming out' the house price, so he doesn't pay a penny more than what you'd accept."

I explained that my friend's listing price may have been perceived as a "reach price," searching for a "stupid money" buyer. The bidder may be gaming out the realtors, who often advise sellers to list high, and take something just below the "ask."

"Why not counter?" I asked my friend, "but offer price guidance through your realtor."

Here's how: Without naming an acceptable price, seller's realtor – whose job it is to buffer the emotions of buyers and sellers – should show the low bidder some square foot comps, citing prices recently paid for similar houses. With this guidance, the low bidder's information is better harmonized with the seller, and they may come back with a higher offer.

If my friend had said: "I'm so insulted by his initial low offer that I won't sell to that guy at any price!" then the seller is letting their emotions overrule rationality; and the seller would risk losing the advantage of a "bid-in-hand."

That bid-in-hand, albeit too low, has some real utility. For instance, if another bid comes in, the seller's realtor can say, all casual-like, "Wow, lots of activity on this listing! Second bid this weekend. Are you sure you're putting your best offer in?"

The same thing can happen when selling a businesses, even though we, as the seller's rep would *never, ever* say a price.

A bidder may offer a low-ball bid, trying to find the bottom. That's quite common. But the seller shouldn't take it personally. Instead, the seller, through their rep (the investment banker or "IB"), should use the bid as leverage with other bidders, just as the realtor did. With a bid-in-hand, the IB will call interested parties, saying: *"This deal is heating up. In fact, I'm looking at a strong LOI right now. Want to get in the game? I'd suggest drafting an offer within 36 hours. Take your best shot early on this one.")*

Next, the investment banker should go back and offer guidance to the low bidder. Show the multiples of EBITDA being paid for other similar businesses, e.g. *comps*. Your IB should have access to databases that show these for recent deals.

Next, use the bidder's pricing logic as a leveraging device. Show that the bidder has the right multiple of EBITDA, it's just been applied to the wrong time period, e.g. last FY as opposed to trailing-12-months.

Next, calculate the *effective buying* multiple of EBITDA after the first year of new ownership, looking out 12 months. If a company is bought at 5X EBITDA, but is growing (which is typical of companies up for sale), the new owner should be aware that a year after closing, with the EBITDA climbing up, they may have purchased it at 4X or 3.5 in a 12-month retrospective. This is very persuasive, often met with a comment like, "Hmmm, that's an interesting perspective."

Finally, offer bridging mechanism to get the buyer to agree to a higher price, without needing to come up with the cash at closing. An earn-out is the most-common tool for this, where an additional sum is paid for the business, often 12 months after closing. A seller's note is common too, where the seller essentially loans the buyer money for the purchase. Earn-outs and seller's notes both reduce the cash-at-close requirements; both are attractive and very common deal elements today.

Bottom line: Don't take low offers personally. It's just the buyer doing what buyers do: *finding the bottom*. Instead, use the low offer as a leverage tool to get the price up, or to signal to other interested buyers that – *Whoa, hot property here, getting lots of attention!* – it's time to get in the game if they are seriously interested.

"One sure thing about luck: It will change." — Asian Proverb

Chapter 37

How Far to Look Back at the Working Capital "Peg?"

As an acquisition closes, the investment banker representing the seller calculates the working capital "peg," or W.C.P., a figure resulting from current assets minus current liabilities, with some exclusions. (A good investment banker actually models the WCP *continually* for the seller long before the closing. But the WCP "peg" is set as the acquisition closes, using the very latest balance sheet numbers.)

Assuming the company is being sold on a cash-free/ debt free basis, let's look at how the WCP is determined, because there are some idiosyncratic exclusions and inclusions when using the very common cash-free/debt-free deal format.

On the current asset side of the ledger, the WCP calculation will exclude "cash and cash equivalents," all of which go to the seller. The current assets include inventory, accounts receivable, and most pre-paids.

For current liabilities, the WCP calculation will include AP, and most accruals.

By subtracting these current liabilities from current assets, you determine the WCP. (In nearly all transaction, there is also a "true-up" adjustment 90 days after the closing, just to double check that these figures were accurate at the closing.)

Note that the value of the inventory is on the asset side of the WCP calculation. A pressing issue in acquisitions today is how far back in time to look when calculating the WCP. When there is volatility of prices, sellers want to calculate the WCP using a trailing-twelve-month (TTM) timeframe, in order to reflect a more normal inventory in the WCP…whereas buyers want to look back just trailing three months, "T3M," to reflect a more normal *current* inventory.

For example, let's say that you have a business that just sells #2 pencils. And say you always carry 100 pencils in inventory, replenishing them as they are sold. For ease of math, let's say you paid $1 for each pencil a year ago. You had $100 worth of inventory on your balance sheet. If the price of pencils doubles over the ensuing 12 months to $2/pencil, you carried the *same number* of pencils, but they had a higher value on your balance sheet: $200. You are likely selling some fraction of inventory at the $2/pencil level, even though your *blended average* for acquiring that pencil was – to your advantage as a seller – less than that.

If the WCP were calculated on a trailing-twelve-month basis, the longer view is to the advantage of the seller, because the seller acquired inventory for less than the value on the balance sheet. (When selling that inventory down, this *price arbitrage* is reflected in higher gross profit dollars, and higher EBITDA, even though the seller is selling the same number of pencils).

That said, if the WCP were calculated on a trailing-*three*-month basis (T3M), it is to the advantage of the buyer, because they are acquiring inventory that they will have to replace at the higher $2/pencil price.

Sellers want the longer view; buyers want the shorter view.

At the 90-day true-up, if the trailing-twelve-month perspective were used, the seller is likely to get an additional check from the buyer, because the WCP would normally be lower than the true-up amount. Conversely, at the 90-day true-up, if the T3M perspective were used, there would probably be less variation between the closing WCP value and the true-up value.

If volatility of prices still in effect, even the trailing-three-month model might not accurately reflect the true WCP. Ironically, when volatile prices start to come off their highs, it may be that the trailing-twelve-month model comes back into favor, but only if it turns out to be more-accurate and fair to both the buyer and the seller.

No matter what model is agreed to, don't treat the WCP as an afterthought. It should be calculated by a qualified CPA, and, as mentioned, it should be calculated on a running basis going into the closing, so there are no surprises for either buyers or sellers as you get close to signing the purchase agreement.

Finally, getting the WCP right has financial implications that reach far beyond just a few dollars either way. As a seller, the advocacy of your investment banker in invaluable in the WCP determination, not only for undertaking the difficult calculation, but for defense of the model used as well.

"Success is walking from failure to failure with no loss of enthusiasm." — Winston Churchill

Chapter 38

Roll-Up Acquisitions: How They Work

I promised myself I would not use the over-used term "synergy" in this column. It was a mighty struggle! See if I won, by reading on.

The term "roll-up" describes a financial engineering process used by private equity and strategic investors, where multiple smaller companies, typically in the same market sector, are acquired and merged.

The goal of the acquirer and participating companies in the merger is to increase the ultimate exit value of each member company and the new company by creating greater *syn...syner...* oh, let's call it *scale*, along with improved market share, and enhancing the ability to deliver cost *syn...syner...* oh, let's call it *savings* that will produce improved EBITDA margins for the combined entity.

These attributes can result in a higher selling price at close for the combined entity, more so than if the companies were sold separately, one at a time, to multiple buyers. Let's say you're selling into a market where companies like yours are selling for 5X multiple of adjusted EBITDA. From the perspective of the original selling prices, the combined entity of a roll-up can sell for an *effective multiple* of 8X or 9X a few years hence, if it performs well.

The typical acquirers of roll-ups are private equity groups ("PEGs"). PEGs will start with a "platform company" and then add "bolt-on" acquisitions to complete their roll-up objectives for a particular market segment, such as retail lumber dealers or truss/component plants. Since private equity groups seek to quickly acquire dominant market share on a regional or national basis, the constituent companies in a roll-up – *once combined* – must represent meaningful market share and improved *syn...syner...* oh, let's call it *profitability*. But, most importantly, it also means that the combined companies will be in a better position to compete and serve their customers with improved purchasing, product offering, marketing programs, and strong financial backing.

The biggest challenge of any roll-up is finding the constituent companies that will be a good fit and that, once combined, will be worth more than its parts. It also means that the companies coming together must understand that some changes will be required to achieve this objective. Those changes could include new unified software systems, new purchasing procedures, new marketing programs, and *syn...syner...* oh, let's call it *efficiencies* to be found in a unified "back office."

Roll-over Shares: There's a catch with roll-ups. The target companies usually don't get all cash for their companies at closing when the roll-up is formed. Sellers will generally be required to put some skin in the game. PEGs often require that a portion of the purchase price be represented by shares in the new company ("NewCo") created by the roll-up. This share type is called "roll-over shares." Often, a minimum of 20% of the deal's value could be represented by roll-over shares. With patience and prudent management, the roll-over shares can become valuable as the NewCo grows over time, potentially with other bolt-ons. As an example, let's say a PEG acquired three independent companies for a total of $45 million. Each owner rolled 20% of the purchase price into the new entity, or $9 million. While the PEG paid $45 million for the transactions, $23 million was equity (a.k.a. cash), and $22 million was borrowed by the PEG, as senior and subordinate debt. In this scenario, because they took roll-over shares (and not all cash for their businesses) the three selling owners combined would own their percentage of 28.1% ownership in the new entity, and the buyer would have a 71.9% ownership. These percentages will change as additional companies are acquired and added in.

Individual Negotiation: The purchase prices for each member are confidentially negotiated with each company. The only entities that need to see a company's financials are the investment banks representing the sellers and the PEG buyers, only sharing the financials once the roll-up is completed.

Roll-ups are ideal for owners who want to stay in the game, but take some chips off the table. They reward those committed to finding *syn...syner...* oh, let's call *collaborative opportunities* and taking a "second bite of the apple" when the PEG sells NewCo down the line.

About the Author

John D. Wagner is a Managing Director for 1stWest Mergers &
Acquisitions, and he leads the technology/ software and industrial
distribution/ building products sectors, as well as the home building
practice. He has been involved with numerous successful private
fund-raising events and merger and acquisition efforts in his career.
John started his M&A career when he served as director of corporate
communications and investor relations for BuildNet, where he
helped roll up 12 supply chain and workflow software companies; he
co-authored the private placement memorandums and an S1 that
raised $147 million for BuildNet from Credit Suisse First Boston,
Robertson Stephens, GE Capital, SSB, and other investment banks.

Recently, John has engaged in the successful sale of a numerous
multi-national software companies, industrial distribution
companies, and lumber and building material retail chains.

A graduate of St. Michael's College (Vermont) and with an MFA
from the University of Alabama, John has most recently been an
adjunct professor in the Business School and the School of

Architecture + Art at Norwich University, where he taught architecture and entrepreneurialism at the graduate and undergraduate levels. Since 1983, John has taught as a professor or adjunct at the university level in the US and in Asia, at numerous educational institutions, including the University of Alabama, St. Michael's College, and Suan Suannatah College, in Bangkok.

He is the author of 21 books – including a young-adult novel and two volumes of poetry; he has written 2,500+ articles that have appeared in such forums as the *Wall Street Journal*, *New York Times*, NPR's *All Things Considered*, *LA Times*, and many other leading trade outlets such as *Industrial Distribution* magazine and *LBM Journal*. John is also president of J Wagner Media, Inc., a leading technology marketing firm (www.WhatAboutWagner.com).

Read more about his background at www.JohnDWagner.com.

About 1stWest Mergers & Acquisitions

With transactions (to date) exceeding $1 billion in deal value, 1stWest Mergers & Acquisitions is full-service, international investment banking and advisory firm that is focused on the lower middle-market of companies with sales of up to $100 million. Established by Founding Partner Ted Rieple, 1stWest has built a highly successful practice assisting owners and shareholders in selling their companies, acquiring businesses, or raising growth capital. With managing directors in the U.S., Europe, Mexico, Panama, Peru, Brazil, Argentina and Chile, 1stWest is uniquely positioned to serve its clients around the globe. Learn more: www.1stWestMA.com

Contact

For mergers and acquisitions engagements, for speaking

opportunities at your events, or for reprint rights to these chapters –

or other future articles – contact John D. Wagner: (919) 796-9984;

J.Wagner@1stWestMA.com.

Glossary of M&A Terms

Here is a list of common terms used in mergers and acquisition. These definitions, obtained through various web sources (all cited below), have been supplemented and added to by the author.

Acquisition: One company taking over controlling interest in another company.

Add-On Acquisition: A strategic acquisition fit for an existing platform/ portfolio company.

Adjusted Book Value: The value that results after one or more asset(s) or liability amounts are added, deleted, or changed from their respective financial statement amounts.

Assets: The property of a business which is defined in an asset purchase agreement, but which generally includes real estate, tangible personal property such as office equipment, manufacturing, automobiles and inventory, as well as intangible assets such as patents, copyrights and trademarks, and may include cash and securities.

Asset (Asset-Based) Approach: A general way of determining a value indication of a business, business ownership interest, or security by using one or more methods based on the value of the assets of that business net of liabilities.

Audited Financial Statements: Financial Statements that have been audited by a Certified Public Accountant in accordance with Generally Accepted Accounting Principles (GAAP).

Balance Sheet: A snapshot of a company's financial condition. Assets, liabilities and ownership equity are listed as of a specific date, such as the end of its Fiscal Year.

Basket: The minimum threshold that must be exceeded before an acquirer is entitled to receive any indemnification payment for losses caused by a seller's breach of representations and warranties.

Book Value: A determination of a company's balance sheet value by adding all current and fixed assets and then deducting all debts, other liabilities and the liquidation price of any preferred issues. (Book value per common share is determined by dividing the book value by the number of common shares outstanding.)

Business Broker: An individual (or company) that solicits and represents business owners that are considering selling their business and acts as an intermediary between sellers (business owners) and buyers. Related uses or terms – intermediary, investment banker. A business broker that represents a seller is often said to be a "sell side rep."

Business Enterprise: A commercial, industrial, service, or investment entity, or a combination thereof, pursuing an economic activity.

Business Valuation: The act or process of determining the value of a business enterprise or ownership interest therein.

Capitalization: A conversion of a single period stream of benefits into value.

Capitalization Factor: Any multiple or divisor used to convert anticipated benefits into value.

Capital Structure: The composition of the invested capital of a business enterprise; the mix of debt and equity financing.

Cash Flow: Cash that is generated over a period of time by an asset, group of assets, or business enterprise. It may be used in a general sense to encompass various levels of specifically defined cash flows.

Closing: The event when the required legal agreements (e.g., stock purchase agreement, asset purchase agreement or merger agreement) are implemented between the parties and shares or assets are exchanged for the consideration specified in the agreements.

Confidentiality Agreement: This is the same as a Non-Disclosure Agreement, see below.

Cost of Capital: The expected rate of return (discount rate) that the market requires in order to attract funds to a particular investment.

Covenant Not To Compete, a.k.a. *non-compete*: An agreement often signed by an employee or a selling shareholder whereby they agree not to work for competitor companies or form a new competitor business within a specified period after termination of employment or the closing of the acquisition. Also called a "Non-Competition Agreement".

Deal Value: The sum of the consideration paid by the acquirer for the equity stake in the target company (plus the value of the net debt in the target, where applicable).

Debt Financing: This is when a firm raises money for working capital or capital expenditures by selling bonds, bills, or notes to individual and/or institutional investors. In return for lending the money, the individuals or institutions become creditors and receive a promise to repay principal and interest on the debt.

Discount: A reduction in value or the act of reducing value.

Due Diligence: A process where a buyer inspects a potential investment. Often includes a detailed review of accounting history and practices, operating practices, customer and supplier references, management references and market reviews.

Earn-Out: A contractual provision stating that the seller of a business is to obtain additional future compensation based on the business achieving certain future financial goals.

EBITDA: A financial term that is a rough proxy for free cash flow. Formally defined as Earnings before Interest and Taxes plus Depreciation and Amortization.

Enterprise Value: Enterprise value (EV) (also called *Total Enterprise Value*, or TEV) is a financial metric representing the entire value of a company after taking into account both holders of debt and equity.

Equity Risk Premium: A rate of return in addition to a risk-free rate to compensate for investing in equity instruments because they have a higher degree of probable risk than risk-free instruments (a component of the cost of equity capital or equity discount rate).

Exit Plan: A strategy, planned or unplanned, to depart an existing situation. The creation of an overall strategy that prepares a business owner and his/her company for the time when that business owner is no longer involved in the operations of the company. Examples of unplanned exits include death, divorce, incapacity, disability, management disputes, influx of competition, technological obsolescence, loss of a major customer, or other unforeseen economic events.

Exit: This occurs when a financial institution, such as private equity firm or venture capitalist realizes its investment in a company. This is usually achieved by selling its stake or by offering the company on the stock exchange.

Exit Multiples:

- Revenue multiple: Enterprise Value / Revenue

- EBITDA multiple: Enterprise Value / EBITDA

- Book Value multiple: Implied Equity Value / Book Value

Family Succession: In family successions or retirement transitions, ownership transfers from passive owners to active family members or outside shareholders. Facilitators are particularly sensitive to estate planning issues, family business dynamics, and the need for discretion and trust to make these transactions seamless and successful.

Fiscal Year: Typically a 12-month period over which a company budgets its spending.

Forced Liquidation Value: Liquidation value at which the asset or assets are sold as quickly as possible, such as at an auction.

Free Cash Flow: The cash generated by a business on a pre-tax, pre-interest basis after making positive adjustments for non-cash expenses such as depreciation and amortization as well as owner-related benefits and negative adjustments for capital expenditures.

GAAP: *Generally Accepted Accounting Procedures* are the common set of accounting principles, standards and procedures established by the Financial Accounting Standards Board that companies use to compile their Financial Statements.

Going Concern Value: The value of a business enterprise that is expected to continue to operate into the future. The intangible elements of Going Concern Value result from factors such as having a trained work force, an operational plant, and the necessary licenses, systems, and procedures in place.

Goodwill: That intangible asset arising as a result of name, reputation, customer loyalty, location, products, and similar factors not separately identified.

Goodwill Value: The value attributable to goodwill. An intangible asset which provides a competitive advantage, such as a strong brand and reputation.

Growth Capital: An investment made in an operating company by an outside investor to support existing or anticipated expansion of the business. May or may not include a change of equity control, but it frequently involves the exchange of equity ownership.

Indemnification: A contractual term whereby one party agrees to compensate the other party for any loss that the other party may suffer related to the contract or transaction. In stock and asset purchase agreements, it is typical for one party to indemnify the other party for a breach of Representations and Warranties made by such party.

Indication of Interest ("I.O.I"): An I.O.I. is often put in place before a formal *Letter of Intent* ("L.O.I.") in submitted. The I.O.I. "puts the cards on the table," to make sure the buyer is in the right ballpark in terms of value to be offered, and how the deal will be structured, e.g. if earn-outs or seller's notes are involved. If the

I.O.I. looks good to the seller, the seller invites an L.O.I., where the offer and terms are more fully spelled out. Sometimes this process is described as "pressure-testing" the offer, to make sure it will hold up.

Intangible Assets: Nonphysical assets (such as franchises, trademarks, patents, copyrights, goodwill, equities, mineral rights, securities and contracts as distinguished from physical assets) that grant rights, privileges, and have economic benefits for the owner.

Intermediary: A merger & acquisition advisor who assists buyers and sellers of privately held small businesses throughout the business transfer transaction process.

Investment Banker: An individual who works in a financial institution that is in the business primarily of raising capital for companies, governments and other entities, or who works in a large bank's division that is involved with these activities. Investment bankers may also provide other services to their clients such as mergers and acquisition advice, or advice on specific transactions, such as a spin-off or reorganization.

Key Person Discount: An amount or percentage deducted from the value of an ownership interest to reflect the reduction in value resulting from the actual or potential loss of a key person in a business enterprise.

Letter of Intent (LOI): A formal, written document indicating the terms a buyer is offering a seller in a proposed acquisition or investment. Although not a contract, it is a document stating serious intent to carry out the proposed acquisition.

Liquidity: The ability to quickly convert property to cash or pay a liability.

Liquidation Value: The net amount that can be realized if the business is terminated and the assets are sold piecemeal. Liquidation can be either "orderly" or "forced."

M&A: An abbreviation for "mergers & acquisitions," which generally refers to the buying and selling of companies, or the combination of two companies in which only one of the companies survives. Acquisitions can be asset purchases, where the buyer purchases the seller's assets, without assuming any liabilities, or stock purchases, where the buyer purchases the business's stock and takes over the seller's business.

Majority Control: The degree of control provided by a majority position.

Majority Interest: An ownership interest greater than fifty percent (50%) of the voting interest in a business enterprise.

Management Buy-out: A process whereby management of a company acquires all or some of the ownership of the company they manage either independently or in partnership with a private equity fund/group (PEG).

Merger: The combination of two or more companies, either through (1) a pooling of interests in which the accounts are combined, (2) a purchase where the amount paid over and above the acquired company's book value is carried on the books of the purchaser as goodwill, or (3) a consolidation in which a new company is formed to acquire the net assets of the combining companies.

Minority Discount: A discount for lack of control applicable to a minority interest.

Minority Interest: An ownership interest less than fifty percent (50%) of the voting interest in a business enterprise.

Net Book Value: With respect to a business enterprise, the difference between total assets (net of accumulated depreciation, depletion, and amortization) and total liabilities of a business enterprise as they appear on the balance sheet (synonymous with *shareholder's equity*); with respect to an intangible asset, the capitalized cost of an intangible asset less accumulated amortization as it appears on the accounting books of the business enterprise.

Net Tangible Asset Value: The value of the business enterprise's tangible assets (excluding excess assets and non-operating assets) minus the value of its liabilities.

Non-Disclosure Agreement: An agreement to protect confidential information being disclosed to a prospective investor or acquirer. Also called an "NDA" or "Confidentiality Agreement" or "CA."

Non-operating Assets: Assets not necessary to ongoing operations of the business enterprise.

Orderly Liquidation Value: Liquidation value at which the asset or assets are sold over a reasonable period of time to maximize proceeds received.

Premise of Value: An assumption regarding the most likely set of transactional circumstances that may be applicable to the subject valuation; e.g. going concern, liquidation.

Private Equity: An investment in non-public securities of, typically, private companies. Also, an investment asset class typically reserved for large institutional investors such as pension funds and endowments as well as high net worth individuals. Includes investments in privately-held companies ranging from start-up companies to well-established and profitable companies to bankrupt or near bankrupt companies. Examples of private equity include venture capital, leveraged buyout, growth capital and distressed investments.

Private Equity Fund: An investment vehicle, typically a Limited Partnership, formed to make investments in private companies via a pool of available equity capital.

PEG: A private equity group.

Portfolio Discount: An amount or percentage that may be deducted from the value of a business enterprise to reflect the fact that it owns dissimilar operations or assets that may not fit well together.

Portfolio Company: A company acquired and owned by a private equity fund.

Promissory Note: A promissory note is a form of debt that a maker/debtor issues to raise money or pay as consideration in an acquisition.

Rate of Return: An amount of income (loss) and/or change in value realized or anticipated on an investment, expressed as a percentage of that investment.

Recapitalization: A financing transaction that allow owners to harvest some of the value they have created in their companies while retaining a large ownership stake in the business going forward.

Representations & Warranties: Statements of fact and assurances by one party to the other party that certain facts or conditions are true or will be true at closing, and often after the closing.

Risk Premium: A rate of return in addition to a risk-free rate to compensate the investor for accepting risk.

Search Fund: An individual or group of individuals seeking to identify an acquisition candidate that the individual or group can acquire and subsequently manage.

Sustaining Capital Reinvestment: The periodic capital outlay required to maintain operations at existing levels, net of the tax shield available from such outlays.

Systematic Risk: The risk that is common to all risky securities and cannot be eliminated through diversification.

Term Sheet: A document setting forth the terms of a proposed acquisition, merger or securities offering. A term sheet may take the form of a "Letter of Intent."

Valuation: The act or process of determining the value of a business, business ownership interest, security, or intangible asset.

Valuation Approach: A general way of determining a value indication of a business, business ownership interest, security, or intangible asset using one or more valuation methods.

Valuation Date: The specific point in time as of which the valuator's opinion of value applies, also referred to as "Effective Date" or "Appraisal Date."

Weighted Average Cost of Capital (WACC): The cost of capital (discount rate) determined by the weighted average at market value of the cost of all financing sources in the business enterprise's capital structure.

Sources:

http://www.DealFirm.com

http://www.MAsource.org/page/Glossary

http://www.MergerMarket.com

https://CorporateFinanceInstitute.com

Notes:

Notes:

Notes:

Made in the USA
Middletown, DE
20 September 2021

47949637R00126